Into the Blue

Into the Blue

by

Virginia McKenna

HarperSanFrancisco
A Division of HarperCollins*Publishers*

FIRST EDITION
SIMULTANEOUSLY PUBLISHED BY THE AQUARIAN PRESS

Library of Congress Cataloging-in-Publication Data

McKenna, Virginia, 1931-
Into the Blue: a book about dolphins / Virginia McKenna.
ISBN 0-06-251005-3
1. Dolphins. I. Title.
QL737.C432M44 1992
599.5'3–dc20   92-52652
                                                    CIP

92 93 94 95 96 XXX 10 9 8 7 6 5 4 3 2 1

This edition is printed on acid-free paper that meets
the American National Standards Institute Z39.48 Standard

Contents

To Bill, our children, and theirs.

With my love

Acknowledgements

This book would not have been possible without the help, kindness and inspiration of many people. Some old friends, some, I hope, new ones.

Lack of space in the text unfortunately prevented me from mentioning everyone who so generously gave me their time and expertise, and revealed to me their personal, often very touching, experiences.

Without the 'Into the Blue' project the book would not exist – and I would first of all like to express my thanks (in no particular order) to the people who were part of it – Stewart Steven, Editor of *The Mail on Sunday*, Graeme Gourlay, Angus Macpherson, David O'Neill and staff at the newspaper; International Fund for Animal Welfare, Bill Johnson and The Bellerive Foundation, Michael O'Sullivan and The World Society for the Protection of Animals, British Divers Marine Life Rescue, Care for the Wild, Dolphin Circle, PRIDE; vets Richard Kock, Deke Beusse, Nancy Logue and Barkley Hastings; Doug Cartlidge, Lucy Maiden, Lee Chanona, Gordon Panitzke, Bev Cowley; the government and people of the Turks and Caicos Islands, Chloe Zimmerman, Dean

Bernal; British Airways Cargo, Anglo Cargo, Linda and Bob Sonderman; Robert Houlton, Sea Life Centres; John Hunt, Elizabeth Emanuel, Will Travers and the team at the Zoo Check office – and many others too numerous to mention.

There are several organizations which have helped me with information and guidance – in particular David Bowles of the Environmental Investigation Agency, Ric O'Barry of Dolphin Project, The Whale and Dolphin Conservation Society, Estelle Myers of The Rainbow Dolphin Centre, Dr Horace Dobbs of International Dolphin Watch, Alvaro Posada Sal Azar of W.S.P.A., Colombia, Greenpeace, Denise Herzing of The Wild Dolphin Project.

Then there are many individuals and societies who really went out of their way to assist me or to contribute to the book and to whom I shall always be grateful. Clare Francis, Peter Hingley of The Royal Astronomical Society, The Royal Botanic Gardens at Kew, Lambeth Palace Library, Dr Paul Bahn, Heathcote Williams, Professor Georgio Pilleri, John Clegg of the University of Sydney, Annette Guck of 3D Gallery, Bristol, the Bill Sammeth

Organization, Olivia Newton John, Clodagh Williams, Joe Phillips, Wade Doak, Joanna Lumley, Patricia Greenhalgh, Cheryl Hutchins, Peter Russell, Dr Nick Gales, Rula Lenska, Kate Carr, Tony Makin, Elizabeth Kemf, Celia Hindmarch of The Alder Centre, Sylvia Berry formerly of The Hillsborough Centre and Angela Thomson.

Most of the paintings and drawings in this book are originals especially created , as is one of the poems – a poignant work by Brian Patten. This has meant a great deal to me. The talents and sensitivity of Michael Foreman, Victor Ambrus, Gary Hodges, Nicky Cornwell, and Susan Richards-Usher visually illustrate and highlight the beauty and character of the dolphin. Julie Morgan and Jean-Luc Bozzoli have also kindly allowed me to include their work. My gratitude also to the publishers of *The Dolphins* by Carol Ann Duffy, Anvil Press Poetry, which was included in their 1985 collection *Standing Female Nude*; to Pimlico Publishing Ltd for *Dolphin Mother* by Pat Moon, from their poetry collection *Earthlines – Poems for the Green Age*, 1991; and to Kate Griffin, widow of Jonathan Griffin, especial thanks for permission to reproduce his poem *Dolphins*, included in the poetry anthology *Headlines from the Jungle*, Viking Penguin, 1990.

On a very personal note I would like to express my admiration for Claire Neal's beautiful design. I could not have wished for anything better.

Finally, my profound gratitude to my researcher Carrie Travers. Without her patience and skill and her good humour when I asked her to find yet another quote, yet another illustration, I would not have been able to complete the book on time. Also to my secretary Sheila Russell who somehow managed to cope with the endless sheets of paper I gave her and to decipher my increasingly illegible handwriting.

And to my family and friends – thank you for your support, understanding and encouragement.

Foreword

Clare Francis

It was a moonless night, dark but absolutely clear. The dome of the sky gleamed with the radiance of a million stars. The gales that had dogged me since leaving Falmouth had abated at last, and the sea was calm. Somewhere just to the south were the Azores, a comforting though unseen presence. Early in the evening a southerly breeze had sprung up, and now *Gulliver G* chuckled happily along, laying her course for America 2,000 miles away. Our progress through the inky water was marked by the most brilliant phosphorescence, which gleamed and flashed like a sprinkling of jewels in our wake.

The night was so perfect, the contrast with the previous conditions so complete, that I put on a tape – Brahms' Fourth – and sat exultantly in the companionway, drinking it all in, thinking: This makes up for everything!

Then my blood froze; my heart leapt into my mouth; I stared in disbelief. We were being attacked! Two torpedoes were coming for us at right angles, very fast and very straight, aiming dead midships. They came on remorselessly, side by side, identical black cylinders whose shape was perfectly outlined by the phosphorescence that streamed from their noses, down their sides and away in long tails behind them.

World War II had been over for almost 30 years: or so I kept telling myself. But another part of me watched in cold fear as the torpedoes came on unerringly, travelling at what seemed like the speed of an express train.

I realized that collision was inevitable. An instant before the impact I tensed and involuntarily blinked.

No explosion, no crash. I looked. There was nothing to be seen. Not a sign. The missiles had simply vanished.

The Brahms had finished some moments before, and now there was an eerie silence. Then, through the sounding-board of the hull, I heard a loud whistle followed by several clicks. I stuck my head down the companionway. More clicking and whistling, very distinct now, and a sound that was almost a whoop. A whoop of what sounded suspiciously like triumph. I leapt up, filled with sudden excitement, and made my way along the deck.

And there the two rascals were, cavorting around the bows! I laughed uproariously as I shook my fist at them. They wove effortlessly across the stem, keeping perfect pace, passing across and under each other with consummate grace. I could almost hear their laughter, and I laughed along with them, suffused by the most intense and exhilarating joy.

After a while they swam off to make another torpedo run – trying to frighten me again, or so I thought. It was only after the third run that I understood the real nature of their game. They were playing chicken. The last one to give way and dive under the keel was the winner. Whatever the rules, the two of them chattered with wild excitement the moment the run was over, exchanging a rapid salvo of clicks and whistles that brimmed with impish delight.

They swam off for a third time. I watched for almost half an hour but they didn't return. In an odd way it didn't matter. It was enough to know they were out there somewhere, just beyond my sight. And enough to remember how thoroughly they had hoodwinked me, which kept me laughing for hours afterwards.

This was my first experience of dolphins, but not my last. In those temperate waters they often came to play around the boat, announcing their presence with the usual stream of clicks and whistles (discussing us lesser creatures, no doubt). If I was in the cockpit I would hear the distinctive hiss of their breathing and hurry to the bows to admire their matchless agility. When *Gulliver* was going fast they would stay a while – how they loved speed! – although to them it was hardly any speed at all. When we were going at a more sedate pace they soon became bored, and who could blame them? Here was a boat-animal that swam at a disappointing rate, in a monotonously straight line, and could neither dive nor play!

They brought with them a sense of enchantment and warm companionship, something that was rare enough in that wide and empty sea. And the fact that they came for no other reason than to play – and with the most unresponsive of playmates – made their visits all the more beguiling.

That they had a lively intelligence, that we shared certain emotional bonds, I had no doubt. That they had something to teach me, I understood only later.

For a while they swam with me – and long after they were gone – they showed me the meaning of pure joy.

Into The Blue reminds us that the relationship between man and dolphin has been a long one and, for the most part, a happy one, and that we have much to learn from these naturally sociable and mutually supportive animals. It also reminds us that in recent years we have sometimes abused our trust, that we have misunderstood the duties of true guardianship, that confinement and exhibition of these far-ranging creatures is nothing but cruel exploitation.

This moving book leaves us no doubt as to where the dolphin and his free spirit really belong. At sea and away – into the blue.

Myths & Legends

...dolphins, shining bright in silver, cut through the
surge, sweeping the sea's surface with their tails

Love animals: God has given them the rudiments of thought and joy untroubled. Do not trouble their joy, do not harass them, do not deprive them of their happiness, do not work against God's intent. Man, do not pride yourself on your superiority to animals; they are without sin.

FYODOR MIKHAILOVICH DOSTOEVSKY (1821–1881)
The Brothers Karamazov

A nature venerated in antiquity,
When this shape-shifting sea sprite
Was Poseidon's messenger, a Gaian pilot...
A demi-god.

HEATHCOTE WILLIAMS
Falling for a Dolphin

Poseidon's messenger
Victor Ambrus

Nestling in the northern hemisphere, near the Great Bear, Swan and Eagle, and 170 light years away from earth, is the constellation of the dolphin – Delphinus. Hundreds of centuries before Christ, this constellation shone down on what the Greeks believed to be the centre of the world, Delphi. It was here that Apollo, the god of light, appeared in dolphin form.

The root of the word dolphin is 'delphys',

which means 'womb'; so the centre of the world was also the womb of the world, and life, light and worship were embodied in the shape of this beautiful sea creature.

We do not understand exactly why the dolphin became so important in legendary, religious and artistic cultures – cultures of huge geographic and ethnic diversity – but that it did is irrefutable. In ancient Palestine, one of the guises of the goddess

Atargatis of Khirbet Tannur was as the dolphin goddess, her headdress crowned by two leaping dolphins.

The influence of Mediterranean religious culture, particularly that of Greece, spread far and wide. All kinds of animals, even those whose natural environment was far removed from desert regions, found their way into temples and shrines and a wide-ranging variety of artistic forms.

Heavenly animals in
Astronomicum Caesareum
by Apianus Petrus,
1540

Even as the Eagles are lords among the lightsome birds or Lions amid ravenous wild beasts, as Serpents are most excellent among reptiles, so are Dolphins leaders among fishes.

OPPIAN
Halieutica II

Some animals, more than others, become a part of our language and our culture – the lion is one. The dolphin is certainly another. Bound up as it was in the everyday religious and legendary beliefs of Nabataean (early Palestinian) civilization, it was accorded another and very special homage. Not only did the dolphin watch over travellers on land and sea to afford them safe passage, it was also believed to help those who eventually embarked on the longer and

uncharted journey 'into the blue beyond of life after death'.

The dolphin is often an intrinsic part of the tragic masks of Persian art, and appears to magnify the belief of the Nabataeans…

… that the dead are really living and that being and not living are themselves so closely united as to be one.

KERENYI *Dionysus u. das Tragische in der Antigone*
(quoted by Goodenough: Symbols VII)

Perhaps modern man no longer places the dolphin in such a deified position (our gods are different), but our fascination for its beauty and character is confirmed in the dolphin's constant representation in art and literature. And, as some people reject the

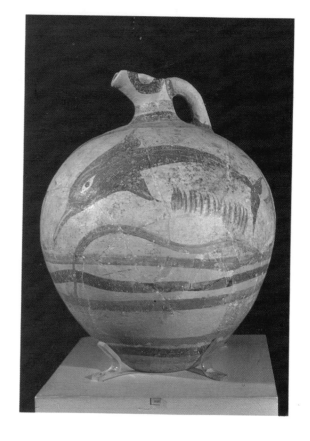

RIGHT A two drachma
silver coin from
Messina, c.500BC

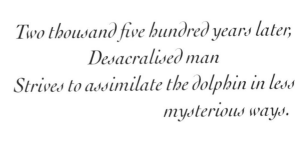

BELOW A four drachma
silver coin from
Syracuse, c.410BC

Two thousand five hundred years later,
Desacralised man
Strives to assimilate the dolphin in less
mysterious ways.

HEATHCOTE WILLIAMS
Falling for a Dolphin

materialistic and scientific mood of the late-
20th Century, they rediscover in the
dolphin a spiritual dimension that reflects
the approach of our ancestors.

Countless stories of humans and dolphins
have come down to us over the ages. They
reveal that those ancient dolphins displayed
the same characteristics of friendliness and
apparent altruism that we recognize in their
descendants. Today, however, those characteristics are differently 'rewarded', and
killing a dolphin is not punishable by death
as it was in earlier times.

Nor do we transform them into stars or
gods.

A leader among fishes.
Line drawing of
Delphinus Turfio

LEFT The dolphin was believed to help those who embarked on the journey 'into the blue beyond of life after death'

BELOW Mosaic in the Queen's Room in the palace at Knossos

Then was there heard a most celestiall sound
Of dainty musicke, which did next ensew
Before the spouse: that was Arion crown'd;
Who, playing on his harpe, unto him drew
The eares and hearts of all that goodly crew,
That even yet the Dolphin, which him bore
through the Agean seas from Pirates view,
Stood still by him astonisht at his lore,
And all the raging seas for joy forgot to rore.

SPENSER
The Faerie Queene

There is more than one account of why the dolphin took that giant leap into the starry firmament, but the most famous is that told by the Greek writer Herodotus in the 4th Century BC. It concerns Arion, a rich musician. Having been away from Corinth for many years, and longing to return once more, he hired a ship and set sail from Tarentum. The Corinthian crew was not to be trusted. Far out at sea, they schemed to dispose of Arion and steal his wealth.

On learning of their plot, Arion begged them to let him sing and play upon his lyre for the last time. Wicked though they were, the crew were eager to hear this famous man's music and agreed to his request. Arion put on the rich costume worn for public performance, the epiporpema, and, standing on the deck, apart from the men, sang a solemn hymn.

When it was over, he flung himself over-board. The story goes that he landed on the back of a dolphin that swam with him to the shore from whence he continued his journey to Corinth.

Arion, his life spared, wrote a thanksgiving hymn to Poseidon, god of the seas, which also mentioned the dolphin's love of music. To reward the dolphin for its love and friendship towards Arion, the gods placed it forever in the canopy of heaven.

RIGHT The constellation of Delphinus, depicted in *Poeticon Astronomicon*, has 10 stars

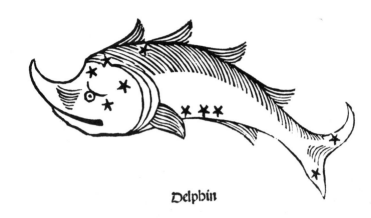

Delphin

BELOW A Ptolemy map featuring dolphins from *Ptolemy Geographia Universalis*, 1540

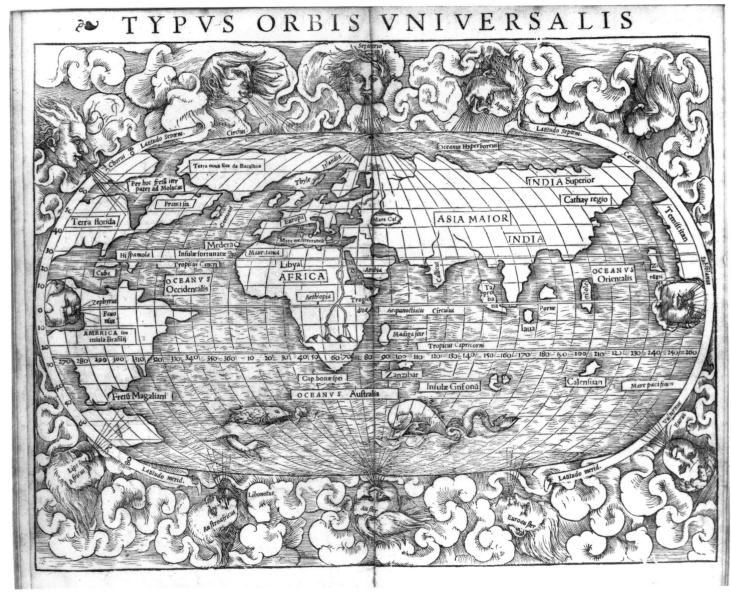

CALECHUT.

LEFT The musician
Arion astride a dolphin.
'Secure he sits and with
harmonious strains,
Requites his bearer for
his friendly pains.' Ovid

BELOW Snub-nosed
hounds with bristling
neck. Detail from
Galatea by Raffaelo

*Highest of the gods, lord of the sea,
Poseidon of the golden trident, earth-shaker
in the swelling brine, around thee the
finny monsters in a ring swim and dance,
with nimble flingings of their feet leaping
lightly, snub-nosed hounds with bristling
neck, swift runners, music-loving dolphins ...*

AELIAN
On Animals XII

LEFT Forever in the canopy of heaven. The constellation of the dolphin as it appears in Urania's Mirror

In Ancient Greece it was thought
That nothing diviner than the
dolphin
Had ever been created.

HEATHCOTE WILLIAMS
Whale Nation

LEFT The Dionysus Plate, c. 530 BC, depicts the god's journey across the wine-dark sea

BELOW Poseidon, god of the oceans, and a dolphin Bernini

A second tale of wicked seamen recounted the plight of Dionysus, the Greek god of wine. When sailing between the Greek islands, he too learned of a plot, to sell him as a slave. Before anything could be done, he transformed the crew's oars into serpents, and his own loins sprouted with vines, filling the craft. He commanded invisible flutes to play and the seamen, overcome with fear, hurled themselves into the sea. Poseidon took pity on them, rescued them from drowning by turning them into dolphins, and forever more, in gratitude, they were at his bidding.

On a rather more down-to-earth note, one of La Fontaine's 'Fables' is the delightful account of a dolphin transporting a ship-wrecked monkey to safety on its back — thinking it was a human being. On discovering its mistake, the dolphin took immediate and (for the monkey) unfortunate action!

BELOW The Oceanus Mask on the famous Mildenhall silver plate, 4th Century AD

The creature sly, seated upon the dolphin's back, Looked very grave and wise; good lack!
Gustave Doré

The Monkey and the Dolphin

It was a custom with the Greeks
For travellers by sea to take
Monkeys and fancy dogs, whose tricks
Would pastime in fair weather make.
A vessel with such things on deck,
Not far from Athens, went to wreck;
But for the Dolphins all had drowned.
This animal is a friend to man:
The fact in Pliny may be found;
So must be true, say what you can.
A Dolphin half the people saves,
Even a Monkey, by-the-by,
He thought a sailor, from the waves
He kindly helped; the creature sly,
Seated upon the Dolphin's back,
Looked very grave and wise; good lack!
One would have really almost sworn
'Twas old Arion, all forlorn.
The two had nearly reached the land,
When just by chance, and such a pity!
Fish asks, "Are you from Athens grand?"
"Yes; oh, they know me in that city;

If you have any business there,
Employ me; for it is truly where
My kinsfolk hold the highest place,
My second cousin is Lord Mayor"
The Dolphin thanked him with good grace:
"And the Piraeus knows your face?
You see it often, I dare say?"
"See him! I see him every day;
An old acquaintance; that is so"
The foolish chatterer did not know
Piraeus was a harbour, not a man.
Such people, go where'er you can,
You meet within a mile of home,
Mistaking Vaugirard for Rome,
People who chattering dogmatise
Of what has never met their eyes.
The Dolphin laughed, and turning round
The Monkey saw, and straightway found
He'd saved mere shadow of humanity;
Then plunged again beneath the sea,
And search amid the billows made
For one more worthy of his aid.

FABLES
Book IV, Fable VII

RIGHT Roman mosaic featuring cherubs playing with dolphins. The Louvre

Perhaps, however, it is stories about dolphins and children that most capture our imagination. The Roman author Pliny the Younger wrote a touching tale of a young boy and a dolphin at Hippo – an African sea town. Here, everyone swam and fished and went out in boats, taking advantage of the tides in the lagoon-like estuary. Young boys in particular enjoyed these activities, and spent hours in swimming races. The winner of the race was the boy who had swum farthest out from shore.

One day, a particular boy – far out in front of the others – met a dolphin that played with him and carried him even further out on his back before returning him to the beach. The boy had been very afraid and told the tale over and over again to the amazed citizens of Hippo. The next day, everybody crowded down to the shore to see what would happen. Duly, the dolphin reappeared and the boy approached it, but, lacking in confidence, soon returned to the shore and his companions.

LEFT Silver coin from Tarentum, Italy, c.460–420BC

RIGHT Boy on a dolphin, 520BC

Several days later, the seafaring community put their fears behind them and ventured out into the estuary, where the dolphin allowed them to touch and caress it. Nobody was happier than the boy who climbed on the dolphin's back and rode with it over the sparkling waves, sensing the feeling of love and understanding between them.

Their relationship grew and although other boys joined in the games, they did not form the same bond with the dolphin as the first boy had done. Indeed, so close were they that sometimes the dolphin would carry his friend to the shore, onto the sand itself, before rolling back into the sea.

Unfortunately, the story does not have a happy ending. The town's peaceful atmosphere was shattered by unwelcome hordes of visitors. The dolphin was put to death. Far ahead, in the future, this story was strangely to be echoed.

A dolphin and anchor sometimes appeared on Christian rings

Cast in bronze
A ceriph of the sea —
A ceriph of the sky
Speeds over mottled cloud.

Hair streams in urchin tufts
A sculptor's son
A human star
            one mortal hand
            on dorsal fin
Arcs, naked down
With concave back —
As you arc up
            A convex wave
Moulded in unseen water.

Whale-tail slaps flat
And water-cleavers cut:

A broad-beak ridge
A fine tight smile-
            A Greek bow strung
            between your eyelet
            eyes.

Your song – his thoughts
Above the traffic soar ...
On frequencies beyond
Our conscious shore.

TOM DURHAM *Boy with a Dolphin*

The inexplicable affinity between man and dolphin, and the animal's association with religious symbolism, continued in Christianity's early years. The dolphin was an emblem of love, of diligence and swiftness in Christian art, and was even used in association with the fish as a symbol of Christ the Saviour. Sometimes the dolphin appears – together with an anchor – on Christian rings, probably as a symbol of Christ on the Cross. On the tomb of a Christian named Redempta there is a vase depicting a dolphin and a dove. The dove symbolizes Redempta's soul, which the

RIGHT The infant Jesus, the Madonna and dolphins Della Robia Andrea, 1435–1525

dolphin is guiding to salvation. It filled the role of the mediator, the intercessor, who saved humans from the 'sea' and returned them to 'land' cleansed of sins.

Although the dolphins that featured in ancient Greek and Roman literature were creatures of the open seas, mention even then was made of another species – the Ganges dolphin, *Platanista gangetica*. This river dolphin had a place in Indian legend, where the constellation Sisumar is described as 'a collection of stars supposed to resemble a dolphin and held to be a form of Vishnu'.

ABOVE RIGHT A lotus with winged dolphins appears on the ship's badge of an Escort Carrier. The motto reads: *Ex aqua in auras* – Out of the water into the air

Miniatures from the
Babur-Nama

The first picture of this animal was found in the unique Persian manuscript 'Babur-Nama', written during the reign of one of the greatest statesmen of the 15th Century, Zahir Ud-Din Mohammed Babur. A highly respected scholar, poet and patron of the arts, his reign produced some of the world's most beautiful miniature paintings. The Babur-Nama is a treasure house for historians, archaeologists, botanists and

zoologists alike. The manuscript contains 96 miniatures – four of which depict aquatic animals.

There is no doubt that the dolphin was worshipped, esteemed and loved in ancient times. The best of human characteristics, and the most wondrous of spiritual aspects, were attributed to it – dolphins helping fishermen, rescuing children from drown-

ing, guiding men to redemption. From time immemorial, humans have found a special relationship with this unique animal. Of course, dolphins were killed then too, and eaten. The Greek army of Xenophon found earthenware containers of salted dolphin meat on the Black Sea coast – but by comparison with their wholesale massacre in the 20th Century, the harmony between man and dolphin remained unbroken.

Kinship is universal. The orders, families, species and races of the animal kingdom are the branches of a gigantic arbour .... Man is simply one portion of the immense enterprise.

J. HOWARD MOORE
The Universal Kinship

The boto of the Amazon
Victor Ambrus

We are familiar with many modern-day abuses of dolphins, but a rather less familiar one is centred on the Brazilian voodoo cult known as Macumba. It concerns the eye and the vagina of the Amazon river dolphin (*Inia geoffrensis*, the 'boutu' or 'boto'). This shy cousin of the Asian river dolphin, which follows fish into 'new pastures' and swims between the trees as the Amazon rises and infiltrates the forest, has been known to rescue people from their capsized boats and to protect people from possible attack by piranha fish.

Although this dolphin is revered by local fishermen, who release it if caught in a net, it is seen as a competitive hunter by commercial fishermen. However, despite the boto's place in traditional legend, the

Eyes of the boto

eye and vagina of this highly endangered species are dried and sold in both South America and Europe. Ostensibly to bring power and a spell-binding sexuality to those who buy them. In 1985, *The New Scientist* described the sale of these 'charms' – not only in markets and stores in Rio de Janeiro, but also by mail order from the *Yellow Pages*.

This now commercialized cult may have had its roots in the legendary stories of Amazonian fishermen, telling of disguised

A delphinium

Ship's badge –
Delphinium

It will live on in the stars. From *Uranographia Britannica* by John Bevis, c.1750

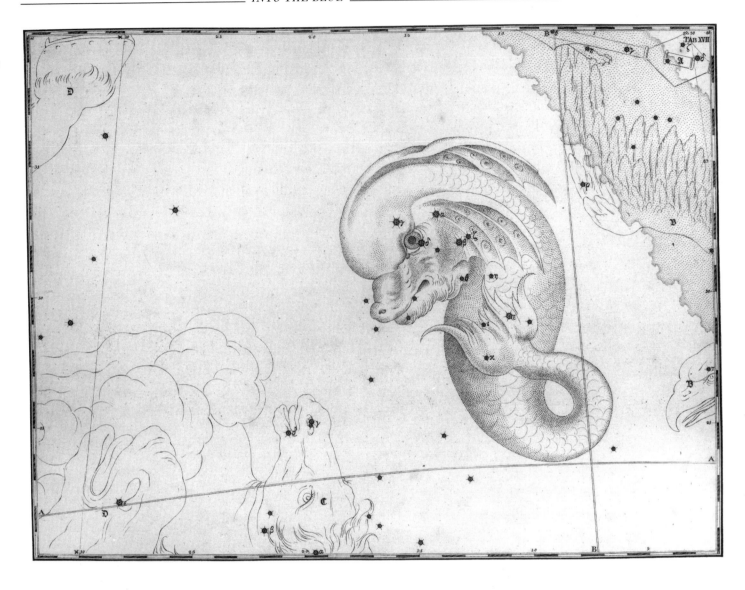

botos coming ashore during village fiestas, and dancing with the village maidens. Subsequently, we are told, these maidens gave birth to a number of fatherless children. But whatever the origin, the demands of this cult market will no doubt hasten the boto's demise. Although, thanks to the gods, it will live on in the stars.

So many gods, so many creeds,
So many paths that wind and wind,
While just the art of being kind
Is all the sad world needs

ELLA WHEELER WILCOX
(1855–1919)

In 1988, Elizabeth Kemf – author and World Wide Fund for Nature representative to the International Whaling Commission from 1982–1991 – visited Vietnam to research a remarkable _living_ legend. In 1991, she became the first person to record a very particular ceremony, and found herself participating in an intensely moving and emotional experience. This is her extraordinary story.

'In Vietnam there is an expression: "He cried as if his father had died". There can be no greater loss or grief. The fisherman who finds a marine mammal washed ashore or who accidentally kills it honours the "mandarin of the sea" with a funeral as if it were his son.

If a dolphin or whale drowns in a fishing net, Vietnamese people in the south of the country give the animals a human burial. So revered are the dolphins and the whales, that their remains are taken to a special graveyard. Three years later to the day, amidst great ceremony, the bones are dug up, carefully washed by the wives of the fishermen and the skeletons reassembled. They are then taken to a special carrier, the same elaborate wooden vehicle used for the burial of humans, and transported by a group of festively dressed pall bearers to the Temple of the Whale.

'Upon arrival of the funeral procession at the Temple of the Whale, the leader of the group, a 12-foot long "dragon", surrounds a colourful column. Fire crackers explode from the top of the column and a troupe of guards dressed in ancient costumes flank a gaily decorated path leading to the stone steps of the sacred site.

'Inside, candles and incense are lit, drums are sounded, and dancers, in blue and orange satin, assemble for the ceremony. Musicians begin playing traditional songs of mourning, while fishermen file slowly into the Temple to pay their last respects. For two days, hundreds of people visit the Temple, praying for the passing of the dolphins' souls from this world to the next. After 48 hours, the bones are deposited, along with the remains of hundreds of other dolphin and whale skeletons, in huge boxes inside the Temple. In 1988, when I first visited the Temple, I wanted to photograph some of the bones for scientific purposes, in order

Washing the bones
at a dolphin funeral

to identify some species that are believed to be rare in other parts of the ocean. I was permitted to photograph the skulls under the close scrutiny of the keeper of the Temple and a curious crowd of fishermen.

'After many visits to the Temple, the keeper and the committee who manage it asked me if I would like to see a human burial of six dolphins. I accepted this invitation immediately and, together with Professor Vo Quy, founder of Vietnam's conservation movement, witnessed and participated in the dolphins' funeral.

'For nearly 200 years, the Vietnamese people have been honouring whales and dolphins in elaborately decorated temples along the coast and in the islands of South Vietnam. All dolphins, whales and seals are considered by Vietnamese fishermen to be princes or mandarins. When they die it is believed their souls automatically ascend to Heaven, where they become "Angels of the Sea in the Sky". All cetaceans are accorded this unique stature by decree of a Vietnamese Emperor in the 18th Century, thanks mainly to a pod of dolphins who helped the Vietnamese navy rescue a group of sailors whose boat was sunk after being attacked by Chinese invaders. According to legend, the Emperor believed the dolphins were responsible for saving the

Funeral procession to the Temple of the Whale

— 32 —

sailors and enabling the Vietnamese to win a strategic battle.

'Present-day fishermen in Vietnam report that dolphins and whales still help them, sometimes warding off sharks or keeping them afloat until they can reach the safety of the shore. For centuries the fishermen have painted the bows of their boats with huge eyes, which they believe dispel evil spirits – and like the dolphins and whales, protect them from the dangers of the sea.'

Those who lose dreaming are lost

ABORIGINAL PROVERB

Aboriginal rock
painting at Kakadu

Travelling to Australia, we enter the land of the 'Dolphin People', a tribe of Aborigines in whose life and culture animals have always played an intrinsic part. The importance of the dolphin to the Wurunjeri tribe is illustrated by their cave paintings – an art form still practised – and by their complex system of communication with wild dolphins that continues today. After a sequence of whistles that passes between the animals and the people, there is a silence in which they speak 'mind to mind'.

Silently communicating with each other, the elders receive guidance from the dolphins on important tribal issues, and from sacred mountain tops, the spirits of the dead return to the wild dolphins in the sea – to be protected in the afterlife as they were in life on earth. The Aborigines feel that while dolphins exist, they themselves are safe. They believe the dolphin to be the animal 'nearest' to the human race and – as did the Greeks – that to kill one would incite the anger of the spirits, of 'the feather-footed man, the Gornge, the executioner'.

The Aborigines still adhere to their traditional philosophies, and some continue to live as a part of the environment. The memorials they have are not man-made. Their spirits live in rocks and trees.

Today, we have almost lost sight of this symbiotic relationship with nature. Destroying, polluting, manipulating and 'managing', we continue to ravage what is left of the earth's and the oceans' riches. Tragically, the warning that we will eventually be left with nothing but a barren and lifeless planet may have come too late.

Although the legends and tales of friendship between dolphins and humans cannot be proved by science, the story they tell is important. It is a story of under-standing, communication and kinship, and the message of this story is being revived today by a small group of people around the world. The legend is living.

Touch the earth, love the earth, honour the earth, her plains, her valleys,
her hills, and her seas; rest your spirit in her solitary places.
For the gifts of life are the earth's and they are given to all,
and they are the songs of birds at daybreak,
Orion and the Bear, and dawn seen over ocean from the beach.

HENRY BESTON
The Outermost House

In the Wild

A coral fairyland Victor Ambrus

See! Where those shoals of dolphins go,
A glad and glorious band;
Sporting amidst the day-bright woods
Of a coral fairy land

P. H. GOSSE
The Ocean (1846)

Victor Ambrus

Don't be surprised, Poseidon, that we
are kind to men. We were men ourselves, before
we became fishes.

LUCIAN
Dialogues of the Sea Gods

There can be few more exhilarating and glorious sights than a 'shoal' of dolphins leaping in unison over the waves, cutting through the air like glistening, curved arrows and leaving behind a trail of rainbow water drops.

Although there are a number of animals with which humans feel an empathy, for many the dolphin's appeal is quite special and remarkable. As we are able to penetrate deeper and deeper into its world, and our knowledge and understanding increases, so our desire to extend our intuitive 'fellow feeling', and to live in harmony with this species, grows.

Water covers nearly three-quarters of our planet, and it is believed that the sea is where life began, about 3 billion years ago. Over many hundreds of millions of years, the various life forms changed. Some creatures left the oceans for the land, and a variety of land mammals evolved. It is thought that the dolphin was one of the small group of land mammals that eventually returned to the sea.

There are about 80 known species of whales, dolphins and porpoises, all belonging to the order of mammals known as cetaceans. The indication that they were once land mammals has been emphasized by looking at the embryonic dolphin in the womb. The beginnings of fingers, minute ear flaps, external sexual organs, and even hair on the head, are all present in the early stages of growth, but have disappeared by the time the dolphin is born in all its stream-lined beauty.

Is there a ghost of an ancestral treaty
For mutual survival
As you shared
And share
This earth's fragile hospitality?

A scrap of your old, reptile brain
Freshly reminds you
That you came from the sea;
That you are composed mainly of water;
That the minerals in the ocean
Are present in your bloodstream
In the same proportions,
Sodium, potassium, chlorine...

For what explains the curious sense of being greeted
by the dolphin
As a long-lost friend?

You meet the dolphin's stare,
The sense of some old alliance rekindled

HEATHCOTE WILLIAMS
Falling for a Dolphin

Nicky Cornwell

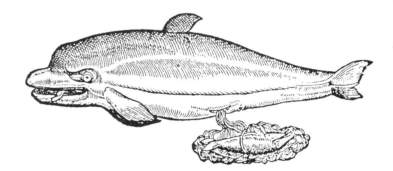

The female Dolphin has breasts like a woman and suckles its young with a a liberal and copious supply of milk. The Dolphin loves its offspring and is an affectionate creature, anxious for its children, and in order to protect them, as with soldiers in line of battle, some are with the front rank, others with the second, others with the third.

AELIAN
On Animals

After she has mated, the female dolphin carries her calf for between 10 and 16 months, according to the species. The baby is born tail first. Within ten seconds, it is pushed up to the surface to take its first life-giving breath. It is helped by its mother – and possibly by other females, 'aunts', which have been in close attendance, providing a caring and protective environment for the new arrival.

Although fully alert and open-eyed from the moment it is born, the little calf will stay near to the mother – sometimes just above her and in front of the dorsal fin. One of its fins may press against her side, enabling it to move with her with little effort. Body contact is very important. The bonding is extremely close; the bottlenose dolphin mother has been known to 'whistle' constantly for several days after the baby's birth – possibly to establish an individual acoustic imprint. Mother and baby may stay together for as long as six years – probably joining another group of other mothers and calves.

LEFT A woodcut by Conrad Gesner from *Historia Animalium*, 1563, depicting the birth of a dolphin calf

LEFT *Mother and baby* Gary Hodges

What a marvel shalt thou contemplate in thy heart and what sweet delight,
when on a voyage, watching when the wind is fair and the sea is calm,
thou shalt see the beautiful herds of Dolphins, the desire of the sea;
the young go before in a troop like youths unwed, even as if they were going
through the changing circle of a mazy dance;
behind and not aloof their children come the parents great and splendid,
a guardian host, even as in spring the shepherds attend the tender lambs
at pasture... even so also the parent Dolphins attend their children,
lest aught untoward encounter them.

OPPIAN
Halieutica 1

Body contact is very important

Coastal dolphins come in close to shore to explore reefs and rocks

As seems befitting the fluid environment in which they live, the social structure and grouping of dolphins is anything but constant.

Although the mother and young remain together, the young sub-adult males eventually leave the female communities and form their own bands. The adult males come and go – ranging far and wide – and have no direct contribution to make to the family unit, except on occasion for protection, hunting and at mating times. This, of course, keeps the gene pool diverse and healthy. Some home ranges may be so vast that it is not always possible to tell where they begin and end; territories and communities mingle and overlap.

The pelagic, or open-ocean, dolphin can travel in groups numbering several hundred – sometimes even thousands. This social structure is very effective when hunting – although the size of the group will usually depend on the available food supply. Using their sonar to keep in contact with each other, dolphins often split up into smaller groups and cover huge areas in search of their prey. When they have located a school of fish they surround it, dive beneath it and, in ever-decreasing circles, finally trap it near the 'ceiling' of the ocean surface. It is a lively and noisy time. Dolphins consume a great variety of food, crustacea and squid, as well as fish, and the coastal dolphins come in close to shore to explore reefs and rocks – sometimes even herding schools of fish up to the beach.

All animals except man know that the ultimate of life is to enjoy it.

SAMUEL BUTLER
Note books 1912

Of all the animals in the world, dolphins seem most wholeheartedly to enjoy life, to leap and play just for the fun of it. There are few more joyous sights than that of a dolphin rising from the sea into the sky in a burst of iridescent foam.

It is an important and popular fact that things are not always what they seem. For instance, on the planet Earth, man had always assumed that he was more intelligent than dolphins because he had achieved so much — the wheel, New York, wars and so on — whilst all the dolphins had ever done was muck about in the water having a good time. But conversely, the dolphins had always believed that they were far more intelligent than man — for precisely the same reason.

DOUGLAS ADAMS
The Hitchhiker's Guide to the Galaxy

As in many species, play provides one of the most vital learning activities for young animals. In dolphins, however, playing appears to continue into adulthood, and seems to express a genuine *joie de vivre*. Leaping, twisting, slapping the water with tail or fin, using the flippers or penis to touch and caress each other – the penis is thought to be used not only for sexual purposes, but as an extra 'arm' to maintain tactile contact within the group – the dolphin's social life is active and affectionate. Their concern and care for each other at all stages of life has been described by many as altruistic.

The Dolphin is believed to love its own kin, and here is the evidence. Aenus is a city in Thrace. Now it happened that a Dolphin was captured and wounded, not indeed fatally, but the captive was still able to live. So when its blood flowed the dolphins which had not been caught saw this and came thronging into the harbour and leaping about and were plainly bent on some mischief. At this the people of Aenus took fright and let their captive go, and the dolphins, escorting as it might be some kinsman, departed.

But a human being will hardly attend or give thought to a relative, be it man or woman, in misfortune.

AELIAN
On Animals V

RIGHT Pursuit of Flying Fish by Dolphins and Birds, a drawing from *The Ocean*, by P.H. Gosse, 1846

Their bodies are shaped like polished, gleaming rockets; nothing protrudes to inhibit the swiftness with which dolphins can streak through the water, dive down to feed, and catapult themselves into the air.

There are a variety of reasons for their dynamic and efficient swimming. The substantial layer of blubber beneath the skin is not attached to muscle, but to a system of ridges to reduce 'drag'. While the dolphins are swimming, the surface of the skin moves in a rippling motion, reacting to changing pressures on various areas of the body. The skin itself secretes a small amount of oil, which can be seen in the shape of a small flat ring on the sea surface when a dolphin has dived out of sight. This is believed to help it discard its dead skin cells and to facilitate the smoothness of its movement through the water.

As an air-breathing mammal, breathing twice in each minute, it has to surface regularly to take in air through the blowhole on top of its head. Some species can plunge to depths of 300m and 500m, and hold their breath for up to seven or eight minutes. Even when racing through the sea, a dolphin can keep up its speed of 17–35km per hour by leaping completely out of the water and breathing in mid-air.

RIGHT Detail from a painting c.520–510BC showing sea birds and dolphins

RIGHT The dolphin has to surface regularly to breathe

And when they have to return from a great depth,
they hold their breath, as if they were reckoning the distance,
and then they gather themselves up, and dart forward like an arrow,
desirous of shortening their distance
from a breathing space.

ARISTOTLE
The History of Animals

Nature, they say, has caused the
Dolphin to be in perpetual motion,
and for the Dolphin, motion ends
with the end of life.

AELIAN
On Animals XI

So, how does it rest, when does it sleep? Not often it would seem – which probably accounts for the fact that so little appears to have been recorded about this function. One of the advantages that dolphins have is that they can just float – or rest – when they want to. They can 'close off' one half of their brain at a time, allowing one side to rest and the other to be alert in order to breathe, which, as a conscious process, is critical to their survival.

*At any rate when in need of sleep it rises and floats up to the surface so that
its whole body is visible, and then goes to sleep.
Even the Dolphin is not unsleeping or devoid of a share of the god of sleep.
At all events when it does sleep it sinks into the depths until it touches
the bottom, and when it reaches it, it wakes on the impact with the floor
of the sea, and rises again. And again when overcome by sleep and subdued
by the god, down it sinks, and again when roused by the impact as before,
up it floats, and it does this time after time, being half-way
between repose and activity, and yet never once does it
lapse into complete immobility.*

AELIAN
On Animals XI

— *52* —

The dolphin has adapted brilliantly to live in harmony with its natural environment

The brain of the dolphin is large, and the area that 'thinks' – the cerebral cortex – is, on average, even larger than the same area of the human brain. However, intelligence should not be related to brain size alone. In any case, should we really persist in comparing animal 'intelligence' with our own? We are, perhaps, alike in very many ways, but we are also very different, and each creature's instinctive behaviour patterns and learned skills have evolved to help it survive in its own particular habitat.

Of course we can say how 'clever' the dolphin is because it can jump through a hoop, or twirl rings round its beak – but that is exploitation of the animal's intelligence, an impoverished behavioural activity meant to demonstrate the expertise of the trainer. The dolphin is surely an example of evolutionary perfection – it has

It can detect you from five miles distant,
Make up its own mind whether or not to appear
And there may be more of its mind To be made up.

HEATHCOTE WILLIAMS
Falling for a Dolphin

adapted beautifully and brilliantly to live in harmony with its natural environment.

The dolphin's large 'thinking' area of the brain is the equivalent part that, in humans, gives us the ability to enjoy art and music. Even more than that, it gives us a *need* for these aesthetic experiences. Dr Horace Dobbs thinks that dolphins use this part of the brain 'to enjoy their environment; the way the sun shines through the water, the way that seaweed waves backwards and forwards, the multitudinous life forms around them…and if you put a microphone into the sea the sounds are utterly incredible…bearing in mind they go up to 200 kilohertz – they go to much higher frequencies than we do, so their audio spectrum is vastly longer than ours. That gives them a feeling of well being which they kind of radiate, and we pick up on.'

They've brains the size of a man's and they like music —
surely make it ... May be exchanging speech?

We (it seems) catch their low
notes only —
        and they, of human music,
            may read more than we know —
firm shapes, shot with elusive depths, of dapples
subtly disturbed by thrusts of arabesque,
            the way a floor mosaic
                mixes its own clear message
in with the high riches, the dappled panels.

Do dolphins stop just short of words? talk music?
Having preferred purity, think in music?

JONATHAN GRIFFIN
Dolphins

In order to understand animals, we have to learn to see the world through their eyes. In the case of dolphins, we need to 'see' the world through their lower jaw and acoustic window. Dolphins 'see' sound. This is not to say that dolphins do not see through their eyes – they see with equal clarity beneath the water and in the air. But it is with sound that they 'see' most clearly, and it is with sound that they communicate with others of their kind.

From observations in the wild, we have learned that dolphin sounds are highly characteristic – individuals and groups are recognized by their special call, and whether they are signals or 'language', each click, series of clicks, squeak or whistle, means something different.

Dolphins 'sound out' their environment with a series of clicking noises. From the echo they receive back as the clicks bounce off various objects in the sea – rocks, fish, anchors, seaweed, boats, or humans – they can 'see' the shape, density and composition of the forms around them. This is their echo-location mechanism.

One clear advantage the dolphin has over us is that it can, in all probability, listen through objects. Sound waves in water penetrate a dolphin or a human being with only the loss of a little reflection and absorption. …A dolphin 'listening' to another dolphin hears the body contours diffusely, teeth and bone somewhat better, and those parts containing air – the alimentary canal, the breathing passages including the lungs, and the air cavities in the skull – quite distinctly.

KARL-ERIK FICHTELIUS & SVERRE SJOLANDER
Man's Place: Intelligence in Whales, Dolphins & Humans

RIGHT The melon – the fatty, oval-shaped organ in the forehead

It returns
To move up and down your body,
Spraying each section of it with a barrage of
  echo-locating clicks;
Penetrating your brain, heart, lungs, stomach, groin,
  legs and feet;
Seeming to gauge each in depth …
Mapping your body's geography
In punctilious detail.
Your brain tingles oddly
As it is spattered, in a second examination,
With unfathomable waves of sound and ultra-sound.

HEATHCOTE WILLIAMS
Falling for a Dolphin

BELOW The boto, the Amazon River dolphin

The susu, the Ganges
River dolphin

So highly developed is the dolphin's sonar, that it can differentiate between different kinds of fish (possibly different colours as well) – and, it is believed, stun or kill its prey with sharp bursts of loud sound. As the dolphin has no vocal chords it is really quite amazing! The sounds are generated within the dolphin's nasal sacs, situated behind the melon – the fatty, oval-shaped organ in the forehead. They are then channelled through the melon and projected outside, in front of the body.

Superb and sensitive echo-location is very important to the river dolphins of the Yangtze ('baiji'), Amazon ('boto'), Ganges and Indus ('susu'). It more than compensates for their minimal eyesight and

enables them to hunt their prey and find their way about in the dim and obscure world of inland waterways.

The river dolphin's physical characteristics are very different from those of its ocean-going cousins. These shy creatures have long, slim, prehistoric-looking beaks, their dorsal fins are much reduced, and they swim more slowly. They have flexible neck vertebrae, unlike the sea dolphins, that enable them to swim in and out of the trunks and roots of trees when the forests become flooded in the rains. The boto, uniquely, chews its food and has bristles on its upper beak and lower jaw – perhaps to prize free crustaceans on the river bed.

Rake marks

Animals live in perfect awareness of each other and in tune with their environment. Unhappily, the planet has become a dangerous place into which to be born, and dolphins can no more escape the threats and perils of today's world than can any other species. Until the pressures and demands of the human race grew to such impossible proportions, dolphins had few enemies. Only sharks and killer whales posed a threat. The scarring seen on the skin of wild dolphins is probably due to skirmishes with these more powerful creatures, although dolphins do 'rake' each other with their teeth when dominance is challenged, or there is a dispute over females. But their agility and courage make them elusive victims, and they live in harmony with most of the other 'finny' inhabitants of the deep.

The hunting of Dolphins is immoral
and that man can no more draw nigh the gods as a welcome sacrificer
nor touch their altars with clean hands but pollutes those who share the
same roof with him, whoso willingly devises destruction for Dolphins.
For equally with human slaughter the gods abhor the deathly doom
of the monarchs of the deep; for like thoughts with men have
the attendants of the booming seas.

OPPIAN
Halieutica V

What would the gods say now? 'Magical animals'. Trusting. Friendly. 'Altruistic'. What do we do to them? And how do we treat them as we invade their territory? We damage and destroy their way of life. We mercilessly hunt them, driving them into shallow waters where they are slaughtered in a blood-red sea with knives and clubs. We kill them with a hand harpoon that resembles the 'cold' harpoon banned by the International Whaling Commission in 1983. Once hit by the harpoon, the animal takes 5–10 minutes to die in agony.

We hack off their fins to supply a demand for so-called aphrodisiacs. We use their teeth as jewellery. We poison them with dangerous chemicals that are emptied, or that leak, into the sea – damaging their reproductive systems. We do irreparable harm to the entire marine environment through the pollution and contamination of the food chain. We disrupt social communities, we separate mothers from calves, causing unimaginable stress and terror.

We catch them – through indifference or by accident – in their tens of thousands in drift nets, where they hold their breath and suffocate to death. We crush them alive as they are dragged through the power blocks of the tuna fishing boats. Those that manage to escape are often maimed, with beaks and fins ripped off.

They are slaughtered in a blood-red sea

LEFT A victim of oil
pollution

RIGHT A Greenpeace diver finds a drowned dolphin in a Japanese drift net

I gave birth to him
In the Warm Waters.
Gently I led him upwards
To where the waters meet the air
And he took his first breath.
Already he knew to stay by my side
And how to suckle my milk.
I showed him how to dive and surface
And to make his breath last.
Six full moons later
He began to catch and eat the fish,
To breach and scatter the tuna.
Already he knew how to leap and dive
For the joy of it.
He hunted and played
With the other calves,
Learning the ways of the waters.

Till the day the boat came.

Too late I saw the nets
Which separated me from him
And the others who were caught.
Too late my signals of warning.

A victim of the nets
Victor Ambrus

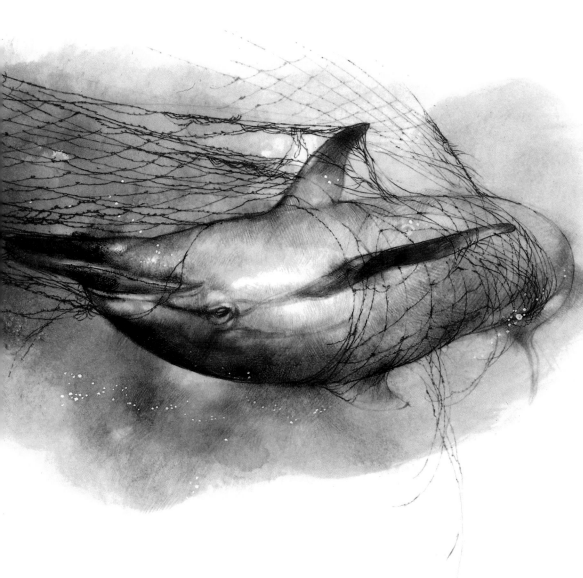

How they struggled to break free.
How they lashed the water.
How they tried to force their bodies
Through the nets.
How they gasped for air.
How their eyes pleaded with us.
How we threw ourselves at the nets
And tore at the ropes with our teeth.
How we cried and leapt
As the great nets rose up.
How great was my agony
As I saw my son writhe in his own.
Could the men not see their pain?

Later we found them
Floating on the waters.
We stayed close,
Sheltering them
And urging life back into their bodies.
But the breath had gone from them
Forever.
And something inside me
Has also died.

Dolphin Mother PAT MOON, 'Earth Lines'

> _Nothing will be left,_
> _Nothing in the air, nothing under the earth,_
> _nothing in the waters —_
> _All will be hunted down, all exterminated._

LEONARDO DA VINCI (1452–1519) from da Vinci's _'Notes'_

Walls of Death

The tuna industry has been responsible for the deaths of _millions_ of dolphins. One-and-a-half million miles of drift nets ('walls of death') are set in a 12-month period in the North Pacific alone. They are made of a very fine, strong material that the dolphins cannot detect or break and it is estimated that since the nets came into use over the past 25 years, at least 9 million dolphins have been killed.

However, there is a glimmer of hope. A United Nations resolution was passed in December 1991 to ban drift-netting by the end of 1992 – although Japan, Korea and all UN countries still using drift nets have been asked to halve their takings by June 1992. This has been agreed, and includes Taiwan, although it is not part of the UN.

In Mexico alone it is now believed that 50–100,000 dolphins may be killed by fishermen every year in the purse-seine nets of the tuna fishing industry. These nets are used where tuna and dolphins swim together, the tuna swimming in schools beneath the dolphin groups.

The two 'British' populations that inhabit the waters of Cardigan Bay and Moray Firth are small and very vulnerable. Like any other coastal species, they are always at risk from propellors, jetskis and from pollution. Noise pollution is another, little publicized, stress factor for the dolphin, as it distorts and interrupts their high-frequency communication system. The incidents of dead and dying dolphins –probably victims of pollution – being washed up on the shores of the Cornish coast have increased alarmingly, and need urgent investigation.

And what of the river dolphins – how do they fare at our hands? They are all classified as either endangered or vulnerable species. In the cases of the Indus and Yangtze dolphins, there are about 500 and 300 left respectively. The Ganges and the Amazon dolphins are doing slightly better, although their predation by humans and the reduction and devastation of their habitat may soon put them on a level with their riverine cousins.

The dangers that confront the river dolphins are similar to those faced by the sea-going species – including netting and pollution. But rivers differ from oceans in that they can be dramatically changed, harnessed and controlled. The dam on the Ganges has prevented the migration of the Ganges susu to nearby river systems. In India, the human struggle for survival is as intense and desperate as for the dolphins, so the dilemma may be insoluble.

The Indus susu has already almost succumbed to human pressures. A reserve has been created for them, which has resulted in a small increase in numbers. Attempts to take this susu into captivity have met with disastrous results. Many die soon afterwards; the longest survivor has lasted five years.

The tonnes of mercury used to purify gold in the Amazon contaminate the river and the unfortunate boto that live in it. Additionally, the ever-increasing number of dams being built compound the boto's problems. Its diet includes 50 different kinds of fish, but because of environmental pollution and change, the diversity of fish species is already in rapid decline.

Lastly – the Yangtze baiji. The most critically endangered of all cetaceans lives in the world's third-largest river. Having once inhabited the whole of the 6,300km stretch of water, the baiji now can be found only in the middle and lower reaches – a stretch of about 1,600km. Its demise can probably be attributed to accidental capture in nets and

RIGHT The critically endangered Yangtze River baiji

イルカ

ABOVE The Japanese word for dolphin

on lines, development, pollution and damage from propellers and craft – rather than from active attempts to kill it.

Many superstitions surround the baiji, but it is considered harmless by the Chinese, and has been accorded a very singular place in China's culture. It has enjoyed government protection since 1975 and is a 'Protected Animal of the First Order'. A semi-natural reserve has been established for the baiji at Tongling and another is planned – both for conservation and breeding purposes. It is a beginning and, in a strange and unusual way, altruistic, which seems appropriate enough.

To all the humble beasts there be,
To all the birds on land and sea,
Great Spirit, sweet protection give,
That free and happy they may live.

JOHN GALSWORTHY
Collected Poems 1934

We must go to them in the wild

Dolphins, like all other wild animals, have evolved to live where we find them, in their huge ocean territory or their dim river worlds. In order to understand them, we must go to them in the wild, not bring them to us. And that, at last, is what is being done by a small but marvellous band of men and women.

With modern, sophisticated recording and photographic equipment, they are penetrating the dolphin's environment and learning the sounds that reverberate in those vibrant aquamarine depths. Wearing sheath-like diving suits that emulate the smooth, velvet-textured skin of the dolphin, and flippers to increase their speed, these 'human dolphins' are, little by little, revealing to the rest of us some of the wonders of the dolphin's life.

Most of us will never be able to enter Neptune's kingdom, but the human dolphins are our story-tellers, our link with our ancestors of old. Through them we can begin to understand more and then we can 'let go', stand on the edge of the shore and gaze out across the shining sea.

ABOVE Recording sound underwater

LEFT An unexpected crumpling of mussel-blue, flippery waves

Every evening a westering sun
laminates the lake-like surface,
a slightly stirred, polished version of sky.
Only an approaching storm
changes it to a rolling sea;

but today an unexpected crumpling
of mussel-blue, flippery waves,
three dolphins buck and pour themselves
out into space, each plunge
briefly expands the gulf's emptiness;

An air-water display,
Interweaving absence and presence,
before they finally dissolve
in a flush of fiddling stars —
Arion has returned for his glittering hoard.

CLYDE HOLMES *Dolphins. Evian Gulf*

Out of the Blue

Ordeal by fire

As the dolphin becomes just another victim of humanity's utilitarian attitudes towards the Earth, it seems as though the ancient friendship between our respective species is no longer entirely reciprocal. Such exploitation is nowhere more evident than in the capture and display of cetaceans for profit. Stripped of their natural identity, deprived of their own culture and environment, the dolphin and whale incarcerated within the oceanarium not only symbolizes an abuse of that ancient relationship, but above all our estrangement from nature as a whole.

PRINCE SADRUDDIN AGA KHAN
The Bellerive Symposium on Whales and Dolphins in Captivity (1990)

Stark unfurnished pools

You are sitting in a stark, unfurnished room; sometimes with two or three other people; sometimes alone. It is a small room – in a few steps you can cross from one side to the other. Four or five times a day you are let out into a larger room, still stark and bare of furniture, where you are made to do a lot of exercises. Always the same. If you do them well you are given a sweet. If not, no reward. You will never leave this place – unless you die or are sent to another building. You are not a criminal. You are there because people more powerful than yourself think you are rather interesting. Never again will you see a tree, touch the earth, climb a hill, smell a flower, choose your friends or lovers, read books, hear music. How does it feel ?

Dolphins in dolphinaria live in stark, unfur-nished pools with companions not of their choosing. Sometimes they are alone. In seconds they can swim from one side of the pool to the other. Four or five times a day they are made to do a lot of tricks. Always the same. If they do them well they are given a piece of fish. If not, no reward. They will never leave these pools – unless they die or are sent to another dolphinarium with the same way of life. They have done nothing wrong. They are there because a species more powerful than theirs thinks they are interesting, and that they will bring in money. Never again will they swim in the vast ocean, leap into the sky, see the shifting light patterns as the sun illuminates the water, feel the currents, hear the miscellany of sounds made by other creatures and moving plants, choose their friends and mates. How do they feel?

I am as a dolphin born
Into a concrete pool,
Who has never known anything better,
Yet yearns for open sea.

Perhaps a seabird's feather
Once landed in my pool,
And instinct knew the odour
Of the place where I should be.

LAURENCE FROST

Sometimes they are alone

The dolphinarium circus industry makes a great play of its role in conservation and education. But who is it fooling? Only itself, and a proportion of the public blinded by the circus razzmatazz that accompanies the dolphin shows – in the same way that it is part of the traditional circus scene.

The circus razzmatazz

The industry's publicity looks convincing. It is not the audience's fault that they are perpetuating and applauding something that is inherently unnatural and unkind. After all, they see the dolphins jumping around, 'smiling', the trainer issuing his commands and the dolphins obeying them. It is fun, the music is playing ... So, what is wrong with that? 'They _do_ get three meals a day' as one tourist reacted. What is wrong with it is that it is totally dishonest, it is _mis_-education. The audience is never told that it is watching deprived animals, stressed animals, animals living totally artificial lives in sterile, concrete 'boxes' so that a handful of people can make a great deal of money.

It is fun, the music is playing... Sea World, San Diego

Animals live totally artificial lives in sterile, concrete boxes

Part of the dolphin show presenter's 'chat' always includes something about the dolphin's physiology and life in the wild; that is the 'educational' bit. And, of course, the point is always made about how lucky these dolphins are because they are not being caught in drift nets or dying from pollution. So – these dolphins should be grateful? Two wrongs do not make a right. We all know that.

Where do the horrors start? In the sea. In the violence of the capture. The American Richard 'Ric' O'Barry is the former trainer of the many 'Flippers' in the famous television series. For the past 20 years, he has been an energetic campaigner against the exploitation of dolphins in marine circuses. He describes what happens. 'You chase them to exhaustion, then surround them with a big net. Their eyes get wild-

…all of the things we inflict on cetaceans in captivity are by definition stressful. Such stress cannot possibly be avoided when the animals are removed from their natural environment.

Dr Paul Spong
The Bellerive Symposium on Whales and Dolphins in Captivity (1990)

looking. The hearts beat fast. You separate mothers and babies. The mothers chase after the boats until they just can't keep up any more.'

Even when dolphins manage to escape, their flippers often get trapped in the nets and tear. Many of them subsequently die from the damage.

For British ex-trainer, Gordon Panitzke, it was the capture that made him have serious doubts about what he was doing. 'We were in a fast speed boat and saw the dolphins in the shallows. We chased them to disorientate them. Then threw out a long net and encircled them and gradually pulled it in. You chose the ones you wanted – as many as you could – 10 to 20 – put them on the boats and took them to the shore. There they were transferred to holding tanks.'

This is how, in 1969, he caught four dolphins – Moby, Lucky, Missie and Baby – for Brighton Dolphinarium. Gordon left Brighton shortly after. When he returned 12 years later, as an RSPCA inspector, all the dolphins had died except Baby. After the trauma and terror of the capture comes the stress of the journey, whether by road or air, to totally foreign surroundings. Strange noises, strange smells, synthetic seawater and a lifeless environment of concrete or tiles. Subjected to injections of antibiotics and sedatives, trained to eat dead fish (which some dolphins never adapt to), it is the start of their new, harsh, man-dominated life. Freedom and choice of any kind no longer exist.

Ric O'Barry in his training days with one of the many 'Flippers'

After the stress and trauma of the journey, the dolphins arrive at the dolphinarium

It is nothing short of torture to take these animals – who are accustomed to the infinite beauty of the open seas, covering vast distances at speeds sometimes reaching 60km an hour – and then imprison them in tiny concrete or metal pools.

PROFESSOR G. PILLERI

Jacques Cousteau, whose experience of dolphins spans more than 40 years, states that: 'The dolphin's life in a pool leads to a confusion of the entire sensory apparatus, which in turn causes in such a sensitive creature a derangement of mental balance and behaviour. Moreover, an inner spiritual crisis is produced by the destruction of the social structure.'

However, this view is not shared by all scientists. Some believe that dolphins in dolphinaria 'flourish', and that the training is something that the animals are eager to

The training pool at Barcelona Zoo

cooperate with. They describe the expertise of blindfolded dolphins that can distinguish between differently shaped objects in the pool and 'exultantly' take back to the trainer the one that elicits a reward. Both interpretations, so conflicting, contain a disturbing hidden agenda of the life and times of imprisoned dolphins.

That dolphins have ever 'flourished' in dolphinaria must be in doubt when you examine those records that exist about their survival after capture. Professor Pilleri (former Director of the Brain Anatomy Institute in Berne), studied captive and wild dolphins for over 20 years. He finally rejected both the invasive and abusive methods of vivisection often required by captive research, and the inhumane incarceration of these fascinating animals.

His report *Cetaceans in Captivity* stated that of the 21 dolphins transported to Europe in 1977, 18 died within one year. In 1978, 33 cetaceans died. In 1979, 17 were imported. All were dead by Christmas. During 12 years at New Zealand's Napier Marinelands, 68 dolphins died – excluding those that died or were maimed during capture. He concludes that the mortality rate for the bottlenose dolphin is 50 per cent after two years, 99 per cent for the common dolphin.

The 1984 Greenpeace report by Dr Susan-Jane Owen reveals that from 1972-82, Japan captured 647 dolphins for 27 aquaria. By 1984, only 293 were still alive.

In the USA, Craig Dezern and Cindy Schreuder state in their report *Dolphins in*

RIGHT The trick is to propel the trainer right out of the water. Windsor Safari Park

RIGHT The pool at Windsor Safari Park

BELOW Humiliation of the dolphins as their teeth are brushed

Captivity that one-third of the dolphins captured or born in captivity in the 1980s are dead, and that since records began in 1973, the animals that died were on average under 10 years' old. This compares to an average lifespan of a dolphin in the wild of between 25–30 years.

In Britain, 300 bottlenose dolphins and eight killer whales have been imported since 1962, although these figures may be an understatement as records have been poorly kept. Today, 11 dolphins remain, including three calves born at Windsor. It is more than likely that the actual numbers of dolphin mortality are very much higher. Factual information is inadequate and the dolphin industry is reluctant to reveal anything that might damage its image.

For example, scientist Dr Margaret

Klinowska's 1985 report on UK dolphinaria (which did not question the dolphinarium concept, but suggested improvement in pool size and 'standards') stated that eight dolphins had been imported to the Animal Training School and Dolphinarium in Wakefield during 1973 and 1974. A document discovered in Florida showed that at least 34 dolphins were sent there. How conveniently some lives are disposed of and forgotten.

As far as the death of calves in concerned, of 150 born in the last 10 years, 80 are dead – most within the first year. The International Zoo Yearbook states that of 134 dolphins born in captivity between 1965–86, 106 died.

To the relief of all compassionate and caring people in Britain, the 30-strong dolphinarium business of the 1960s had been reduced to just two by 1991. In America, however, 40 new dolphin 'parks' are on the drawing board. This would bring the total to 73. Many USA animal welfare groups are desperately trying to prevent more parks being opened, but in the case of commerce versus compassion, the outcome is, perhaps, predictable.

The Australian government has taken a very positive approach. The conclusion of its 1985 enquiry on animal welfare stated that 'the benefits of oceanaria in Australia for humans and cetacea are no longer sufficent to justify the adverse effects of capture for captivity'. It recommended that no new facilities for captive cetacea should be constructed, no further catching of wild cetacea should be allowed, and that the importation of cetacea from abroad should be banned. This does not mean that the dolphinaria that still exist in Australia are free from problems – far from it.

By themselves, however, statistics can seem meaningless. What matters is that each individual that makes up the total sum is a living, breathing animal. A creature that feels pain, frustration, grief, aggression – emotions that would be a normal part of the animal's daily life in its natural environment. Emotions that are spread over, and diffused by, the constantly changing social and structural make-up of the environment itself.

But remove this creature from its rightful home – put it in an inhospitable, unsympathetic cage – subject it to the stresses and disciplines of transportation, training, performance and captivity – and these emotions will become distorted and exaggerated. Only in captivity has an orca,

Reprinted from the
DAILY TELEGRAPH
22nd February 1991

Killer whales drag trainer to her death

by John Hiscock
In Los Angeles

THREE killer whales bounced a screaming trainer around a pool before dragging her to her death in front of horrified spectators at a marine park.

The 20-year-old woman had ridden on the back of one of the whales during a show at Sealand of the Pacific in Oak Bay, British Columbia, but then she fell as she walked along the edge of the pool.

As she was helped out, one of the whales seized her foot and pulled her back into the water. For the next 10 minutes the whales knocked the screaming woman around the pool and then dragged her under the water.

"The whale got her foot and pulled her in," said Nadine Kallen, one of the onlookers.

"They were there the minute she fell in. They started bouncing her around. She went up and down three times.

Mr Al Bolz, Sealand manager said "They were just playing. It was a tragic accident."

a killer whale, been known to show hostility towards a human being. Only in captivity are there signs of stereotyped and neurotically aggressive behaviour and stress-related illnesses. In captivity there is no escape from the intensified hierarchy in the pool, or from the exigencies of training and the relentless repetition of performance.

Doug Cartlidge began working with dolphins in the very early days of the industry. He found them 'magical' animals. There were only about five qualified trainers in those days, but dolphins were being transported in droves from Florida, dumped into holding pools and tanks and receiving a quick training course before being dispatched elsewhere to satisfy the greedy demands of the dolphin entertainment impresarios. The travelling dolphin show soon became a familiar part of the circus scene – both in Britain and abroad – with the helpless animals being bundled from place to place on stretchers in beast wagons.

Cuddles, the killer whale at Flamingoland, was very ill and receiving day and night care from Doug and his staff. The Bank Holiday weekend was looming and Cuddles was due to be moved to Dudley Zoo – in time to attract the holiday crowds. Dudley had no dolphin pool – Cuddles would be in an area that was part of the moat. However, this seems to have been of little concern to those responsible for the exercise. The killer whale died soon after its arrival at Dudley Zoo. Doug Cartlidge resigned.

In 1974, Doug went to Seaworld in

Queensland, Australia. Although the dolphins were captive, it was 'better'. There was no concrete, there was natural seawater, and fish came and went so the feeding was at will. The stress factors were less, but the dolphins were isolated for punishment purposes.

As with Gordon Panitzke, it was taking part in a capture that finally made up Doug's mind to leave the industry. 'We used to capture our own dolphins out there, and when you start ... you are the person who is taking them. When you see wild dolphins they are so fluid, so relaxed – we change them when we bring them into captivity.'

*Behind the stage lurks an anticipated, ruthless and profit-seeking business,
which nevertheless some scientists actively support.
With cold-blooded cynicism, they attempt to prove that dolphinaria
have an educational benefit by giving people contact to these creatures
of the sea and encouraging love and respect for them. It was no different
with the human slave trade...Today, the slave trade is undoubtedly
regarded as one of the darkest chapters in human history.*

PROFESSOR G. PILLERI

Behind the stage at
Windsor Safari Park

BELOW A reward for tricks well done

Do we really believe that watching dolphins wearing funny hats and glasses, jumping through hoops, pulling boats, being used as water skis, made to 'sing' 'Happy birthday to you' actually teaches us something? Even if it did, can we condone the punishment that awaits these animals if they refuse to perform, or perform inadequately? As Ric O'Barry says, 'The trainers call the method "Positive Reward." I call it "Food Deprivation." Captive dolphins are controlled by hunger.'

Doug Cartlidge adds: 'The tricks are not performed because the dolphins enjoy

One of the punishments if they are not working properly is to lock them away on their own. You put them in a pen and ignore them

doing them. First you find out how much they'll eat and still work. After that you condition the dolphin to associate certain hand signals with certain tricks that will result in the dolphin getting fish. You then find out if they are loners or prefer company, because one of the punishments if they are not working properly is to lock them away on their own. You put them in a pen and ignore them. It's like psychological torture.'

In the 1970s, the training by starvation system was carried to extremes. An extract from Brighton Dolphinarium's notes during a 10-day starvation period stated 'She's looking a bit thin, but that's only to be expected because we've reduced her food.' Two days later the dolphin started to work. The trainer added 'We've broken her.'

The show is over – the crowds go home

World is what you swim in, or dance, it is simple.
We are in our element but we are not free.
Outside this world you cannot breathe for long.
The other has my shape. The other's movement
forms my thoughts. And also mine. There is a man
and there are hoops. There is a constant flowing guilt.

We have found no truth in these waters,
no explanations tremble on our flesh.
We were blessed and now we are not blessed.
After travelling such space for days we began
to translate. It was the same space. It is
the same space always and above it is the man.

And now we are no longer blessed, for the world
will not deepen to dream in. The other knows
and out of love reflects me for myself.
We see our silver skin flash by like memory
of somewhere else. There is a coloured ball
we have to balance till the man has disappeared.

The moon has disappeared. We circle well-worn grooves
of water on a single note. Music lost forever
from the other's heart which turns my own to stone.
There is a plastic toy. There is no hope. We sink
to the limits of this pool until the whistle blows.
There is a man and our mind knows we will die here.

CAROL ANNE DUFFY
'The Dolphins': Standing Female Nude

Suicide in the wild has been observed only when animals panic during capture. So stressful is life in a dolphinarium for its inhabitants that there have been several instances of animal suicide. Jacques Cousteau witnessed this when two of his captive study animals hit their heads continuously against the side of their pool. He ended his captive investigations.

The suicide in his arms of one of his favourite dolphins, Kathy, abruptly terminated Ric O'Barry's long association with the dolphinarium industry. On returning from a trip, he received an urgent phone call to go to the Seaquarium. He 'went straight to Kathy's pen to find her floating lethargically in the water. There were big black blisters covering her entire body. I jumped into the pen with her and she swam right into my arms. And she died right there. I remember crying out "My God, what have I done?"'

Kathy had decided to stop breathing.

No aquarium, no tank in a marineland, however spacious it may be, can begin to duplicate the conditions of the sea. And no dolphins who inhabits one of those aquariums or one of those marinlands can be considered 'normal'.

JACQUES COUSTEAU

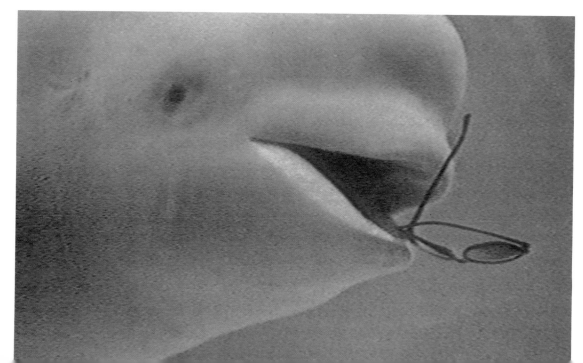

Before we leave the dolphin circus industry, I want to mention something that – even in its name – appears so delightful: 'The Petting Pool'. If you opened up the stomach of a dead dolphin that had been in a petting pool, would you be surprised to find coins, balls, hats and a variety of other non-food objects? Would you be surprised to find that the dolphins had 'dark, puckered holes where the eyes should be'? Would you be astonished to learn that the chlorine content is even higher than in the ordinary dolphin pools because of the accumulation of faeces in the small pools, and the hundreds of

The petting pool at Sea World in San Diego

hands that are constantly being put in the water? Well, surprising or not, this is the reality for dolphins in petting pools.

Reduced to becoming indolent, lethargic beggars in their sun-glare prisons from which there is no respite, the dolphins move slowly as the visitors ply them with sardines and pat them – and occasionally molest them. Still sticking to their chant about 'education', the American mega dolphin business appears to see no wrong in this sickening treatment of one of nature's most beautiful and sensitive animals.

When a thing exists which you really abhor, I wish you would remember a little whether in letting it strictly alone you are minding your own business on principle, or simply because it is comfortable to do so.

JOHN GALSWORTHY
Much Cry – Little Wool

Those members of the public who are distressed by such matters often find it difficult to speak out – understandably. But when a situation is deeply offensive, nothing will hold them back – as happened in the case of the Miami Seaquarium. So incensed was one visitor by what she saw that she wrote to a newspaper: 'The specter of these dolphins, born to roam the seas, with an intelligence many marine biologists compare with ours, haunts me.' The institution had... 'abused its prized residents'.

Fortunately for the animals, more and more people are prepared to be uncomfortable. It is the only hope left.

Mona Lisa of oceans.
Your sunshine smile beguiles
Enchants and gathers us
Into your silver-sprayed
Arc-en-ciel.

In ocean or pool your joy
Blinds us to your secrets.
Your glistening beauty,
Your tolerance of us —
Who also hide behind a mask of mirth —
Pierce the hearts of some who watch
The chlorine-scented show,
Far from the dolphin's deep and distant home,
Light years from its origins
In nature's amphitheatre.

They say the elephant weeps salt tears.
The dolphin, creature of salt expanses,
Conceals its pain.
Locked in its smile as hopelessly
As we have land-locked it,
In concrete worlds of artificial sea.

VIRGINIA McKENNA

It would appear that the main pre-occupation of scientists continues to be with the dolphin's method of communication. More specifically, how they can communicate with us. An American neurologist, Dr John Lilly, was so dedicated to the understanding of dolphin 'intelligence' that he carried out some appalling investigations in order to further this ambition. One reported experiment required electrodes to be inserted into the brains of living dolphins – a process which entailed driving holes into their skulls with a hammer.

Lilly's obsession with establishing a mutual 'language' started when he slowed down the recorded sounds made by dolphins – which he decided resembled human speech. He then tried to teach the dolphins English. They learned a number of words that somewhat resembled 'bye-bye' and 'stop it' – both highly suitable under the circumstances. But in 1969, Lilly ceased his experimentation as five of his animals committed suicide. It seems somewhat ironic that as the quick familiarity with the dead walls of the concrete pool reduces, and sometimes eliminates, the dolphin's use of sonar, so the scientists try to introduce a totally artificial communication process, for *our* benefit!

Nature is a sort of art sans art; and the right human attitude to it ought to be, unashamedly, poetic rather than scientific.

JOHN FOWLES
Animals (US) Vol 13 Part 9

Never believe that animals suffer less than humans. Pain is the same for them as it is for us. Even worse, because they cannot help themselves.

DR LOUIS J. CAMUTI (1883–1981)
Park Avenue Vet

Pain is the same for
them as it is for us

In 1980, Dr Lilly returned to continue his work, again to investigate communication and language, with two dolphin 'students' called Joe and Rosie. There is little published on the results of this work, but a happier future awaited Joe and Rosie – to be revealed in the final section of the book.

Thankfully, Lilly finally became aware of the suffering and deprivation his research was causing the dolphins. He rejected his method of investigation and became totally converted to the pursuit of knowledge in the wild.

We blindfold dolphins to show the efficiency of their echo-location system. We put probes in the larynx and nostrils to examine movement during sound production. We train them to push buttons and levers, to choose between balls of steel or wood, red or blue. We teach them to speak English. Why?

The only way scientists should study dolphins is to swim with them in the wild. Only then can they properly understand what the dolphin and its life are really like.

Whenever an animal is somehow forced into the service of men, every one of us must be concerned for any suffering it bears on that account. No one of us may permit any preventable pain to be inflicted, even though the responsibility for that pain is not ours. No one may appease his conscience by thinking that he would be interfering in something that does not concern him. No one may shut his eyes and think the pain, which is therefore not visible to him, is non-existent.

ALBERT SCHWEITZER

Who is to say that you are in sole charge of evolution?
That you are the be all and end all
Of this particular planet's experiment in self-awareness?
Only you.

HEATHCOTE WILLIAMS
Falling for a Dolphin

No skipping off for a quick feed
Victor Ambrus

The bottlenose dolphins continue to smile as they float, confined, in their 24 x 24 ft pens at the US naval bases. They smile as they feel the pangs of hunger before the training sessions begin, and before the reward for work well done is distributed. They smile as the orange 'anti-forage' devices are clamped around their beaks—no skipping off for a quick feed. They can never stop smiling. That is their tragedy.

Of 62 'navy' dolphins, the survival rate averaged less than six years – as opposed to 25–30 years in the wild.

There are now about 100 dolphins on US naval service. How long will they survive? We may never know. What they do and how they live is definitely top secret. Activities like retrieving items from the seabed and guarding ships seem harmless enough, but what kind of objects do the dolphins retrieve, and what kind of ships do they guard? There is no doubt that the motive behind the use of dolphins in war is not harmless at all. Not least to the dolphins themselves. Whether in their role as guards or as carriers of explosives.

It appears that both Russia and the USA are the countries primarily involved with this kind of ocean secret service operation. But who knows— the secrets are so closely guarded and one can understand why. The 1990 Greenpeace book on dolphins contains a comprehensive and researched account by Dwight Holing of this area of dolphin exploitation.

As trainers of dolphins in the dolphinarium

No sooner does man discover intelligence than he tries to involve it in his own stupidity.

JACQUES COUSTEAU

industry have left the business because they could tolerate it no longer, so have trainers of naval dolphins. They are disgusted not only by the idea of teaching these naturally friendly and trusting animals to become potential killers, but also by their treatment during training. A number of trainers have revealed that some of the animals had been mistreated – kicked and beaten. Those that had escaped, about 20 per cent, still had the anti-forage devices on their beaks, so they would have starved to death. They were being trained to attach explosives to the bottom of enemy ships, and – in what is called the 'swimmer nullification pro-gramme', where a long, hollow hypodermic needle is fastened on to the beak – they were trained to inject compressed carbon dioxide into enemy frogmen, which forces the men's internal organs out through their body orifices.

Once again, the dolphin's natural expertise and intelligence has been ruthlessly harnessed for the purpose and politics of the human race.

How is an animal, which for centuries has only been recorded for its intelligence and friendliness towards man, now taught by one man to kill another? They must use electrical stimulation of the pain and pleasure centres of the brain in order to induce and reward aggressive behaviour. Of all the depraved and disgusting activities of which man seems capable, this one in particular must rank highly.

DR FAROOQ HUSSAIN, King's College University, London

The few weeks of freedom enjoyed by Brightness the Beluga whale, following her escape from a Russian research facility, are at an end. Lassoed from Turkish waters, her future, we are told, will be in a Russian circus. Her brightness will soon be dimmed

They cannot ask for kindness
Only for mercy plead,
Yet cruel in our blindness
Which does not see their need.
World-over, town or city,
God trusts us with his task,
To give our love and pity
To those who cannot ask.

EDGAR A. GUEST (1881-1959)
Obligation

People & Dolphins

A recognition from time past

*The Knowledge that all things are one and that one thing is all things —
Plankton, a shimmering phosphorescence on the sea and the spinning
planets and an expanding universe, all bound together by the
elastic string of time.*

STEINBECK
Log from the Sea of Cortez

It is easy to forget what is written so clearly above. I, myself, had forgotten for a moment about the oneness of nature, that we should have reverence for all life. It is easy to become 'carried away' by dolphins, to become overwhelmed by their beauty and by what we call their intelligence. By the apparent willingness of a few solitary dolphins to seek out human company, to befriend us, and by their seeming ability to 'understand' us and to 'sense' our true nature.

It is perhaps easier for most people to relate to, and feel sympathy for, a lion, a bear, an elephant or a dolphin than a lemming, a vulture or a snake. But we have to dig a bit deeper into nature's melting pot and try to understand all the ingredients that make up the harmony of the natural order of life and death. The writer Jan Morris vividly reinforced this important concept for me.

'I live on the northern shore of Bae Aberteifi, Cardigan Bay in Wales, and now and then I see, leaping far out at sea, the one group of dolphins that survives in these waters. The glorious slate schooners that used to sail out of Porthmadog have all gone; I hardly see an ocean-going vessel from one year to the next; yet still the dolphins plunge out there, like creatures of another world.

'When I point them out to tourists, generally from the English Midlands, I am often patronizingly disbelieved. Impossible they say, there are no dolphins around here, it's probably fish, or birds, or bits of flotsam –"you're seeing things, love". However when I finally convince them a strange thing happens to these prosaic visitors from the interior. A kind of glow comes over them. They stand rooted there, staring. They take no more notice of me, as I steal away, but seem lost in wonder, as though they are seeing something magical.

Creature of another world
Victor Ambrus

Dolphins in Cardigan
Bay, Wales

RIGHT A ship's badge
featuring one of Nereus'
fifty daughters, or sea
nymphs, all of whom
became attendants of
the sea god Poseidon

'Alas, only the dolphin, I think, can have quite this effect upon them; and though it is marvellous indeed that this creature has so endeared itself to humanity, and impressed itself upon the dullest imagination as something enchanted and enchanting, still I think there are object lessons to be learnt from the infatuation. Because the dolphin is friendly to man, because it has a quaint and amiable personality, because it seems always to be smiling, because it is clever and clean, it is no more worthy of our concern than any other creature. All living things, it seems to me, are equal in the eye of nature (or of God), and they should be equal in our eye too. If we should think twice before harming a dolphin, we should think twice before harming a rat.

I want to realise brotherhood or identity not merely with the beings called human, but I want to realise identity with all life, even with such things as crawl upon the earth.

MOHANDAS KARAMCHAND GANDHI
(1869–1948)

'That we have to harm rats sometimes seems to me self-evident – every creature fights off its predators. But a dying rodent is no less sad than a dying dolphin, and the spell that the animals of the bay casts upon its watchers all too often blinds them to a wider truth; that it is no more than the spell of nature itself, to be respected in all its limitless glory, beautiful and ugly, amiable and bad-tempered too. What a day it will be when those tourists, inspired by the spectacle and returning to the car, resolve not after all to squash the bloody fly that buzzes around their windscreen, but to put it safely out of the window instead!'

Some believe that the dolphin's affinity with our species, and their sensitivity towards us, is a kind of kinship that originated when all life began and emerged from its birthplace in the ocean; that our relationship with, and feeling for, the dolphin is unique, stemming from a deep-seated recognition from time past.

Certainly, the cooperation between dolphin and fisherman cannot be denied. In early Greece and Italy, the eastern coast of Australia, Burma, Florida, the coast of Mauretania and the rivers of the Amazon, from the distant past until the present day, people and animals have worked together to effect their catch.

Detail from a painting c.520–510BC showing dolphins and fishermen working together.

There is in the province of Gallia Narbononsis ... a lake known by the name of Latera, where dolphins fish in company with men ... at stated seasons of the year innumerable multitudes of mullets make their way into the sea ... the fish immediately make with all speed towards the deep water which is found in a gulf in that vicinity, and hasten to escape from the only spot that is at all convenient for spreading the nets. As soon as ever the fishermen perceive this, all the people ... shout as loud as they can, and summon Simo to the scene of action ... sooner than you could have possibly supposed, there are the dolphins, in all readiness to assist. They are seen approaching in all haste in battle array, and, immediately taking up their positions when the engagement is about to take place, they cut off all escape to the open sea, and drive the terrified fish into shallow water. The fishermen then throw their nets, holding them up at the sides with forks, though the mullets with inconceivable agility instantly leap over them ... At last, when the capture is now completed, they devour those among the fishes which they have killed; but being well aware that they have given too active an assistance to be repaid with only one day's reward, they take care to wait there till the following day, when they are filled not only with fish, but bread crumbs soaked in wine as well.

PLINY'S *Natural History* Book IX

Arms of the Worshipful Company of Fishmongers, c.1512. In heraldic symbolism, the dolphin is regarded as pre-eminent among fish

So well did the Aborigines and porpoises understand each other that the blacks laid claims to individuals in the same way they do with dogs, and it was death by the law to kill or injure any of these. They have a very keen sense of hearing, and it was by this means that the natives were enabled to call them from a distance of a quarter of a mile or so when their services were required to drive a school of fish into the shallow water, where they could be taken with the tow-rows (scoop nets) or hand nets.

J. HALL
Coastal Archaeology in Eastern Australia

I am not sure if the fishermen's friend Simo (snubnose) was always so generously rewarded, but such happenings have been widely documented, and each story has its own character.

Some cooperative practices have continued in precisely the same way for over 140 years. In Laguna, southern Brazil, about 40 fishermen put out their nets every month. The circular nets are edged with weights and carried by individual fishermen who stand in a line in the shallow water of the lagoon and wait for the dolphins to arrive.

Because the water is so dark and cloudy, the men cannot see the fish and must wait for the dolphins to give them the sign to cast the nets.

Gradually the dolphins approach. All at once, one will surface in front of a fisherman and turn on its side. That is the sign the fisherman has been waiting for and the catch begins. It seems that the hunting strategy is led by the dolphins – on which the men are completely dependent. The dolphins' reward is not bread soaked in wine, but a good feed of about 10kg of mullet!

Any relationship between a wild animal and a human can, for the human, mean a whole new approach to life. To be trusted and accepted by a wild animal is an experience that no cynic can minimize or destroy. Sadly, the possibility of entering a wild animal's territory and establishing a rapport based on love and trust is remote.

However, some have been fortunate enough to enter the dolphin's world, to observe, to study and even to form relationships. Not only scientists and experts, but many 'ordinary' people as well. The growing fascination for this animal is leading to an awareness and appreciation of the unique and complex life force of cetacea, and the mysterious and unfathomed environment they inhabit. Maybe we are responding to deep-seated emergency signals within ourselves, compelling us to regain our true perspective.

For many, certainly, the dolphin is a messenger, sent to inspire us to live in harmony with nature – and ourselves. Almost without exception, the people I have met who have swum with wild dolphins have told me that it 'changed their lives', uplifted them, that it was a 'magical', 'mystical', or 'healing' experience.

Entering the dolphin's world

It is no doubt a mistake to attribute to (animals) all human feelings, but equally it is surely a mistake to deny that there is a common thread joining all living creatures.

LORD GRIMOND

LEFT Nicky Cornwell

RIGHT Shaka and Jojo

BELOW MIDDLE Dean and Jojo – two dancers in total harmony

There are several ways you can meet dolphins. You can swim with friendly, solitary, wild dolphins, with captive dolphins in 'swim programmes' in America, and even with groups of wild dolphins.

I have swum, for an all too brief 45 minutes, with Jojo, an amicable wild dolphin in the waters of Providenciales, an island in the Caribbean. I was with my son, Will, five other people, and a black dog called Shaka. The sky and the sea were crystal clear – of a blueness that you usually see only on postcards and gaze at in disbelief. As we travelled along quite near to the coast, Dean Bernal – a young American who lives in Providenciales and who is the National Parks Warden – pointed out a dark fin moving through the water about 500 yards away:

'There's Jojo!'

We slowed down and within seconds the dolphin was up to the boat. We put on our

masks and snorkels and jumped into the water. So did Shaka!

We had been asked not to touch Jojo, but somehow that was irrelevant. Just to swim in the water with a wild dolphin, to be accepted, was enough. It was so beautiful, and peaceful, and funny! The dog was paddling away, his black legs going nineteen-to-the-dozen, and below him 'standing' on his tail and looking up at these busy legs was Jojo. Squeaking and clicking for all he was worth! When Jojo had had

enough, he swooped down to the ocean floor and foraged for food – followed by Dean who was like a dolphin himself. I watched the two of them twirl and dive and circle each other, like two dancers in total harmony. It was a joy to see.

There is a special bonding between Jojo and Dean that started in 1988 and that has developed over the years into a unique relationship of mutual trust. However, it would be misleading to imply that wild dolphins accept everyone that swims their way. Jojo has been known to bite people who tried to impose themselves on him. We do not like complete strangers assuming we are close buddies either!

To the dolphin alone nature has given that which the best philosophers seek: friendship for no advantage. Though it has no need of help of any man, yet it is a genial friend to all, and has helped man.

PLUTARCH

From the translucent waters of the Caribbean, we move to New Zealand, travelling back in time to the end of the 19th Century. Many accounts have been written of the dolphin called Pelorus Jack who, for about 24 years, escorted ships to the safety of harbour through hazardous rocks and currents. The fullest account was by John Robbins of Earth Save, who revealed that Pelorus Jack's expertise and goodwill in guiding ships through the dangerous passage was nearly brought to an abrupt end right at the start.

The first people to sight the dolphin were the crew of the Boston schooner *Brindle.* Their instinctive reaction was to kill Pelorus Jack, but the captain's wife managed to prevent them. So his role as 'pilot' began.

Some time later, a drunken passenger on board a ship called the *Penguin* shot at Pelorus Jack, gravely wounding him. The dolphin, his body spurting blood, disappeared from view and the enraged crew almost killed the would-be assassin. The *Penguin* went on its way unaided and nobody saw the wonderful dolphin guide for several weeks.

Then, one day, he returned and resumed his task once more. The only ship he never helped again was the *Penguin* which, as fate would have it, was wrecked one day as it endeavoured to navigate the turbulent waters and many of the crew and passengers were drowned.

Pelorus Jack
Victor Ambrus

The story of the dolphin at Hippo in Myths & Legends was, as I said, to be strangely echoed centuries later. One day in 1955, a lone female dolphin appeared in Hokianga Harbour in the North Island of New Zealand. The first to see the new arrival was a Maori fisherman who recalled that the dolphin energetically leapt and splashed around his boat. Two months later, it appeared again when the fisherman Piwai Toi was out in his boat with friends. This time, the dolphin followed them back to the harbour.

'Opo' seemed to prefer the company of children – in particular that of a gentle 12-year-old called Jill Baker. The dolphin would always seek her out, swimming with her, and eventually allowing Jill to touch her. Sometimes the dolphin would go between the girl's legs, lifting her up and swimming with Jill on her back. Opo earned the nickname of Opononi Jack as she loved to be around boats, playing with the oars and often guiding craft between two points on the shore.

The activities of the dolphin were recorded regularly in the press for several months, and – as at Hippo – the tranquillity of Opononi, the remote northern town, was completely shattered.

When the crowds and the traffic grew to extraordinary proportions, sometimes 1500–2000 people a day, the residents of Opononi became very apprehensive and concerned for the dolphin's safety. She had received some wounds from propellers and some visitors behaved rather roughly towards her; indeed, boatloads of tourists seemed to compete vigorously for Opo's attention – each trying to attract her to its own position. However, these incidents were rare and the general atmosphere of the crowds that gathered to watch and be with Opo was peaceful and happy.

The public's repeated requests for the legal protection of Opo were brought into force on 8 March 1956. Too late. She was found dead on 10 March, her body jammed between rocks five miles away from the Opononi beach. At first it was thought that she had been trapped by a falling tide, but doubts soon began to spread. Her body was damaged, and it was known that some locals had been disturbed and angered by the volume of vehicles and visitors to the area. Subsequently, the dolphin's death was attributed to a gelignite explosion – although whether this was accidental or deliberate has never been proved.

Apart from those residents who had become disenchanted with the Opo scene, Opononi's inhabitants and, it seemed, most of New Zealand, were in mourning for the dead dolphin. Many tears were shed and flowers strewn on the grave. Letters and telegrams arrived from all over the country. Nobody grieved more deeply than Jill Baker – Opo's sweet and loving friend. Some years later, a monument was erected in memory of the friendly dolphin – depicting her carrying a boy on her back.

LEFT The monument to Opo at Opononi

RIGHT *Sometimes Opo allowed Jill to swim on her back*
Michael Foreman

Ride little boy
On the back of a dolphin
Ride
In a sea of blue

Laugh as he swims in the waves round the island
With the sky like a jewel
Over you

Glide on a lazy afternoon
In the sun, boy;
You'll have travelled miles and miles
Before the lovely day is done, boy.

Ride little boy
On the back of a dolphin
Watching the sea birds above you there

They'll call your name
Little boy on a dolphin
You're one with the sun and the sea and the air.

He'll take care of every hair
Of your head, boy;
And he'll bring you safe to shore
When it's time for you to go to bed, boy.

Ride little boy
On the back of a dolphin
Ride
Far away little boy.

Boy on a Dolphin
a song by ELIZABETH COUNSELL

A handblown crystal
dolphin bowl
by Malcolm Sutcliffe

Underwater pyramid
Jean-Luc Bozzoli

Where once there was a sandy track, unspoilt bush country and a caravan site, now there is tarmac, a hotel and all the outward, visible signs of a thriving tourist industry.

Monkey Mia (the word 'mia' is Aboriginal for 'home' and 'Monkey' was the name of the ship that sailed here in the 1830s) in Western Australia, is famous all over the world. Long gone are the days of Aboriginal simplicity and 'dreamtime' music, although archaeologists have discovered signs of a 1000-year-old settlement in the dim recesses of a cave. The Aborigines would sit on pristine sands or fire-red earth and communicate with their 'cousins' in the shimmering sea, undisturbed by the chatter of crowds and the roar of vehicle engines.

The peace of those days has vanished, but something still remains – the human desire to communicate with creatures in the wild. More difficult perhaps when you are one of a possible 200,000 people to visit Monkey Mia in the course of a year, but for each individual a personal watershed. All these people come to see a community of dolphins – a changing, breeding group of wild dolphins that come and go as they please. That they please the human visitors is unquestionable!

It all began in the 1960s when a fisherman and his wife were living on their boat at Monkey Mia. It was a hot, sticky night and Mrs Watts had got up as she could not sleep. She heard a dolphin splashing around the boat and, without thinking, gave it a piece of fish. The dolphin took the fish and came back for more – this time accepting it from her hand. They called the dolphin Charlie. In due course, he brought his family to the boat – and so began the long-running saga of the dolphins at Monkey Mia.

Then, at the beginning of 1989, a little six-week-old dolphin calf died. A few weeks later, two more. Then adults disappeared, never to return. Was it pollution? A disease transmitted by humans? A toxic substance in the fish? There was intense speculation. No bodies were washed up on shore and, to add to the mystery, the problem seemed to relate only to visiting dolphins. The group of some 200 inhabiting the bay appeared healthy and normal. No one has ever solved the enigma.

For each individual, a personal watershed at Monkey Mia

Monkey Mia

Three years on, the surviving dolphins have been joined by others as they visit the shallows. Tourists continue to pour in. Scientists carry out dolphin behavioural research. Dolphins and people still meet. Lives are 'changed'. Humans become more sensitive, aware. Feeding or not, the dolphins can come and go at will. They choose who they want to make contact with, they make their feelings known. For once, they hold the hoops.

Dolphins
Julie Morgan

*When you swim with one he is
constantly aware of your health and
well-being, of your physiology and
the level of your emotional arousal.
There is no hiding or lying and no
possibility of denial.*

DR LYALL WATSON
Gift of Unknown Things

*The betrayal of even one false thought,
    you're prone to feel —
And it could stave in your body
With a lackadaisical flick of its fin;
    Torpedo into you at thirty knots,
Snapping your spine as if it were a sardine's;
Crush each limb into fragments with its jaws,
And eighty-eight needle-sharp conical teeth.
But it appears to entertain no such wish.*

HEATHCOTE WILLIAMS
Falling for a Dolphin

Dolphins do not know who you are – king,
statesman, peasant or pauper. The dolphin
responds to the person. As we use X-rays to
penetrate our bodies visually, the dolphin
'hears' through us, 'sees' our heartbeat, our
state of anxiety, anger, tension – or our
peace and tranquillity.

And your mind feels recharged by the
nameless wildness of this creature,
So stretched that you effortlessly
think of it as a person,
Of your two minds blending,
Your mind reaching out, becoming
one with another

HEATHCOTE WILLIAMS
Falling for a Dolphin

Freddie

The dolphin called Freddie lives in the sea
around Amble on England's windswept
northeast coast. He has been visited by
many people over the past five years.
Friendly to most (he puts the 'show-offs' in
their place!), he appears to respond in a
very specific way to the nature and needs of
various swimmers, heavily disguised in
their wet suits, goggles and flippers.

Angela Thomson is a very pretty 16-year-
old from Liverpool. On 7 March 1990, she
was walking home with her identical twin,
Sharon, when Sharon was killed by a passing car. Angela suffered deep depression
and grief. Not only had she lost her sister,
she had also lost the 'other half' of herself.

Sharon's parents and Angela all received
counselling and support, but it was proving
overwhelmingly difficult for them to come
to terms with Sharon's death. Almost all

Dolphins 'smile'
Its face is permanently engraved with this subtle,
        potent smile,
As if a smile were the only facial gesture worth making,
And it had therefore settled into a genetic trait:
The emblem of its seductive ability
To disarm a fellow-creature —
Whom it should have been persuaded
Was its most intractable enemy —
By the only safe method; making friends.

HEATHCOTE WILLIAMS
Falling for a Dolphin

Angela with Freddie. 'I just wanted to be with him.'

Angela's experiences had been closely bound with Sharon's – she had little identity as herself – and therefore it was vital that she should build up new experiences that would allow her to be an individual in her own right.

It turned out that Angela had always longed to swim with a dolphin, and her social worker thought that swimming with Freddie might help her to overcome her grief. Freddie swam round her all the time, very near: 'It was incredible – I didn't think about anything else at all, it was just him and me in the water, like my best friend. I felt a bit selfish – I just wanted to be with him. When I touched him it was unbeliev-able – very soft and warm.'

The swim with Freddie meant so much to Angela that she went again. Freddie would leave others and go to her. On the second trip, Freddie would not go near the boat unless Angela was in the sea.

Shades of Opo and Jill.

For Angela, swimming with a wild dolphin allowed her to take the first steps on the road to a new and very different life. Freddie had worked his 'magic'. Angela was 'recharged'. She had 'let go'.

'Time loses all meaning – you just feel, literally, spaced out, as if you have jour-neyed to a far country.' So wrote psy-chotherapist Kate Carr in her diary after swimming with Freddie, the culmination of a 20-year-old desire to swim with dolphins. '"He's coming to you," cried the watchers in the boat, and, sure enough, there was this dark grey, graceful torpedo homing towards me and I was totally unafraid. Considering how frightened I am of horses and bulls – even cows – I was quite prepared to be scared of this huge mammal, some 12 feet long, in his natural habitat. But I wasn't.'

Kate had read about some of Freddie's habits, so she was not at all surprised or concerned when '...he turned underneath me, his long white belly uppermost, at right angles to me, so that we made a cross in the water, and he slipped his little thin whippy pink penis between my thighs just above my

Have you swum with a friendly dolphin
When the day dawns clear and bright,
And seen his welcoming leap of joy,
As you leave the harbour and pass the buoy?
That's pure delight.

Have you swum with a friendly dolphin,
Dozing under the noonday sun,
And stroked his belly, so smooth and strong,
Or felt your body being towed along
In elfin fun?

Have you swum with a friendly dolphin
In the sunset's fiery glow,
When every wavelet is tinged with gold,
And his silhouette, so huge and bold,
Is a graceful bow?

Have you swum with a friendly dolphin
As the silvery moon rides high,
And ocean and earth are bathed in white,
And the dolphin's aglow with a phosphorous light,
As he glides by?

Have you swum with a friendly dolphin
In the North Sea's rolling swell?
Or a choppy squall, as a cloud passed by,
And a leaden greyness darkened the sky,
And raindrops fell?

Have you swum with a friendly dolphin
And a boatload of friends of a kind?
The harmony linking you all, and him,
As you tumble out of the boat for a swim –
It blows your mind.

Have you swum with a friendly dolphin
And known your panic allayed?
Be it ladders, or snorkels – whatever your fear –
Perhaps the ocean's depth; once the dolphin's near
You're not afraid.

Yes, I've swum with a friendly dolphin
In the moonlight, the sun and the rain;
And the varying moods of the ocean swell
And my life will never – I know full well –
Be the same again.

KATE CARR *The Dolphin*

left knee, and towed me gently but steadily, in big circles, away from and around the boat ... Every now and then he would leave me, to go away for a breathe, and then come back again, belly uppermost. I laughed and laughed with joy, and gazed up at the blue sky and the puffy white clouds ...'

Making friends was what it was all about.

People are disturbed not by things but by the view they take of them

EPICTITUS

Some controversy – and a subsequent court case – surrounded Freddie recently regarding the apparent sexual stimulation of the dolphin by one of his visitors – Alan Cooper – a well-known opponent of keeping dolphins in captivity. The supposed 'incident' was brought to the public's attention following comments made by Peter Bloom, the owner of the dolphinarium at Flamingoland.

The fact that dolphins use their penis as

another 'arm' in interaction with their own species, as well as ours, has been recorded on innumerable occasions. It is also widely known that dolphins are highly sexual animals, and that copulation in the wild is part of a behaviour pattern not necessarily allied to the reproductive urge. In 1989 Horace Dobbs wrote:

'In July there was a dramatic change in Freddie's behaviour, prior to which he was friendly and curious but allowed only fleeting contact. He quite suddenly started rubbing himself against those in the water, often hooking the backs of their legs with his extended penis. Not surprisingly some were startled by this behaviour, whilst others were frightened or amused. This close physical contact was quite indiscriminate and depended

Horace Dobbs
swimming with a
dolphin called Simo

Rula Lenska swimming
with Freddie

upon the sensitivity, not the sex, of the recipient. Any embarrassment was soon forgotten when it was realized that dolphins are uninhibited sensual animals. Indeed, such behaviour has been observed frequently with other friendly male bottlenose dolphins and is regarded as a gesture of trust.'

The maligned swimmer was cleared by a unanimous verdict. It showed, amongst other things, how little we understand about the natural behaviour of animals – however much we profess to do so.

The actress Rula Lenska is well known for her love of animals and her condemnation of their persecution and mistreatment. In 1983, she swam with some dolphins at Atlantis dolphinarium in Australia, and enjoyed the experience of being so close to the dolphins in the pool. As with so many of us, she did not realize then what it meant to the dolphins to be snatched from the wild and subjected to the stresses of captivity and performance. She also spent a day with the dolphins at Monkey Mia.

In 1991, however, she swam with Freddie. 'I couldn't resist going to meet Freddie. It was wonderful though freezing cold. ... No fish – no rewards – just curiosity and friendship.' Rula now believes that it is completely wrong to imprison dolphins in any way. Human contact is fine, providing the dolphins can come and go at will. For her, swimming with Freddie had 'a magical, mystical effect on the soul'.

Freddie is a free, wild dolphin. He is not artificially fed; he comes and goes as he pleases and interacts with whom he chooses. He likes some people more than others. One day he may decide to leave – it is entirely up to him. In March 1992, he was seen swimming near Tynemouth – far from his home range at Amble – before disappearing into the North Sea. He has since been seen again, but nobody knows whether or not he will return to his Amble friends to resume his old way of life.

There is a holy book – the sacred manuscript of nature – the only scripture that can enlighten the reader.

INAYAT KHAN

Emerald Mermaid
Susan Richards-Usher

Swimming with dolphins, both in the wild and in controlled circumstances, is a controversial issue for many people, and provokes opposing views. Some do not agree with it at all. Others consider it an indispensable lifeline. So much depends on the individual's level of expectation.

This aspect has been vividly described in an article by Peter Russell, writer, philosopher and consultant. I feel totally in tune with what he says.

'The most moving encounter occurred this summer with a lone dolphin who had become separated from its family group, and had befriended a small fishing village in Ireland. Setting off at the earliest opportunity, I spent three glorious days learning from one of the most sensitive and caring beings I have ever had the privilege to meet. I say "learning" deliberately, for this dolphin taught me much in that time.

'Rather than my taming a wild animal, it seemed very much as if the dolphin were taming me. It seemed as if the dolphin knew my feelings. Perhaps it did. With their highly developed sonar, dolphins can "see through" the skin, sensing the shapes and movements of our inner organs. Perhaps it "saw" my inner trepidation as clearly as we see the frown on a person's face. Whatever the reason, it moved around me with a care and precision that gradually taught me there was nothing to fear. It seemed to respond to me with a deep empathy. I felt cared for in the way that we care for our closest friends and family. Yet this dolphin had never met me before .

'Throughout this taming, and my learning to let go of fear, another lesson was taking place; learning to let go of wanting; whenever I was looking for the dolphin, wanting her to be with me, anticipating her appearance, she was not there. Only when I had let go of all desires and expectations did she suddenly appear.

'One time, believing that she was far away, I took the opportunity to explore a crab pot buried deep down in a bed of seaweed. So absorbed was I in discovering what was inside, that I did not at first notice another head next to mine, apparently equally intent on seeing the contents.

She suddenly appeared, made contact, and disappeared again

We cannot talk with (animals) as we can with human beings, yet we can communicate with them on mental and emotional levels. They should, however, be accorded equality in that they should receive both compassion and respect; it is unworthy of us to exploit them in any way

REBECCA HALL
Animals are Equal

'Another time, I decided to swim to the shore. I wanted to say goodbye in some way, and inwardly willed her to come by. But nothing came of it. So letting go of my desires, I decided to leave anyway. A few yards from the shore she suddenly appeared, made contact, and then disappeared again.

'This learning to let go of wanting was for me a reflection of something I am continually having to learn in my life upon the land. With the dolphin this lesson was brought home in an unavoidable way. Helpless in the water, there was nothing much I could do to manipulate the world the way I wanted it to be. All I could do was let go.'

At first glance, 'swim programmes', where captive dolphins are required to respond to strangers entering their pool four times a day, seem to be fine for everyone. Dolphins and humans alike. The humans have a wonderful 'experience' and children with learning and speech problems are stimulated to the point of actually saying words. There is no doubt that for the *humans* the benefits appear considerable.

What about the dolphins? First of all, they are captured from the wild. They have no alternative but to be there and, in some facilities, the same reward system prevails as in the dolphinaria – even tricks can be part of the programme. Although the situation is described as 'elective captivity' there doesn't really seem to be much choice as far as the dolphins are concerned. They are conditioned to remain in the lagoons or the pens. They are fed. If – as happened in

one centre – a few jump over the low fence between the lagoon and the sea, they are soon rounded up and brought back again.

Swim programmes are big business. Up to $60 for a 20-minute session is the general fee, although $125 is sometimes charged. Big business means that more people will want to join the burgeoning industry. Hotels are getting in on the act – two dolphins have already died in the Hyatt Regency Waikoloa Hotel in Hawaii which opened in 1988. Most important of all, more and more dolphins will be captured from the wild.

There are hundreds of people who will take part in swim programmes and not be aware of these concerns, or feel any of their own. They are so excited and thrilled by the proximity of this 'wild' animal, so elevated by the experience, that what it means for the

dolphin does not occur to them. In the same way that riding an elephant in a zoo arouses no uneasiness about the elephant's problems – nobody thinks they have any.

David Wills, Vice President of investigations for The Humane Society of the United States, swam with dolphins in one of the swim programmes. He wrote:

'The swim was a highlight in my life; one that left me charmed, in love and paradoxically saddened. For the single inescapable fact of that wonderful time was that while I was free to swim with the dolphins, they were not free to swim with me ... willing perhaps, but not free. And that is the moral issue that condemns all captive dolphin swim programmes. No arguments can justify the forced confinement of these unique and complex individuals. Their lives without their freedom is a sad and prolonged slavery,

no matter how velvet the chains nor how kind the jailer. Someday, I would like to swim with dolphins again, but it would have to be with their consent – consent given freely to swim with me in the open freedom of their natural environment; on their terms, not just mine.'

Those are my feelings exactly.

There are little 'islands' of human/dolphin encounters dotted all around the world. Hawaii, Brazil, the Bahamas, Australia ... oceanic gatherings where small groups of people meet small or large groups of dolphins. Spinners, spotted, bottlenose – each species with its own behaviour patterns, each individual with its own character and 'personality'. Some of the people are scientists, some are not. All are there to watch and wonder, to learn and to enjoy.

The environment is difficult and unpredictable, and presents even more challenges for the observer than a rainforest or a desert. Dark and deep, ever-changing, translucent blue or stormy, and often impenetrable, the sea's secrets are not easily uncovered. But the people who take out their boats in search of knowledge know that this is the only way to explore and understand the dolphin mind.

Pushing through green waters
Symbol of joy
You leap from the depths
To touch the sky
Scattering spray
Like handfuls of jewels.

Not caged by union rules
Unfettered by sales targets
No trains or planes to catch
Your time is set by the flow
Of the sea's tide
And the moon's glow.

You give us images of ecstasy
That we lock away
Behind the doors of memory
For quiet moments
When released by our possessions
We dream of a freedom like yours.

HORACE DOBBS *Dolphin*

Into the Blue

Man's best friends Catherine Havard

In a world where so much that is wild and free has been lost to us, we must leave these beautiful mammals free to swim as they will and must. They do us no harm. They wish us none, and we should leave them alone.

RICHARD O'BARRY
Behind the Dolphin's Smile

The rehabilitation of captive animals to the wild is a difficult, risky and expensive process. It is rarely undertaken and not always successful. The wealth of publicity surrounding a handful of achievements is a reminder of how scarce such successes are and how little we really have to congratulate ourselves about.

There have been some dolphin releases over the years that did not attract the attention of the media. One of the earliest concerned two dolphins called Liberty and Florida, set free in 1973 near the island of Eleuthera (Greek for 'freedom'), east of Nassau. There was no post-release monitoring period but Ric O'Barry thinks that the dolphin that turned up 12 years later in the Turks and Caicos islands – and now called Jojo by the islanders – may be Liberty. It cannot be proved, but it's a nice idea.

The first dolphin release to attract significant attention concerned Joe and Rosie; the two dolphins that had been part of Dr John Lilly's 'communication research' programme for seven years. Captured in 1980, the animals had mastered a 'vocabulary of 40 word-whistles', but interspecies 'dialogue' was never achieved. The project folded and, with Ric O'Barry in charge, it was decided to try to return Joe and Rosie to the ocean.

Joe and Rosie

They were first taken to The Dolphin Research Center at Grassy Key in Florida, where Joe and Rosie were to taught to forget everything they had learned in captivity. This involved teaching the dolphins that fish were essential food, not just rewards for doing a trick and that the sound of a whistle (sometimes heard from another part of the centre where trainers were working with other animals) was not a sign for them to start performing. When the dolphins were readily eating live fish, they were transferred to an ocean pen off the island of Georgia, where the water was clean and rich with a variety of fish and crustacea. Finally they were released into the ocean. They have been sighted 15 times since the summer of 1987, and on one occasion Rosie and another dolphin were seen swimming with two calves.

The Five **R**'s for Dolphins: **R**escue, **R**ecuperation, **R**etirement,
**R**ehabilitation and **R**elease

WILL TRAVERS _The Born Free Foundation_

Rocky, the solitary dolphin at Morecambe Dolphinarium

For Rocky, the solitary dolphin at the run-down dolphinarium in Morecambe, the five **R**'s began to be formulated in 1989. A young woman called Bev Cowley had visited the pool expecting to find two dolphins. Instead, she found only one, Rocky. His former companion, Lady, moved there from Whipsnade, had become pregnant and had died from toxaemia one month earlier. She had continued to perform until her death. Watching the pathetic show, Bev decided to do something for Rocky – to bring to an end his 19 years in a concrete box – only a few dolphin leaps away from the smells and sounds of the open sea.

The number of local people opposed to the dolphinarium grew from six to 300, and eventually the campaign attracted nation-wide support. Media interest was intense, and the daily peaceful picketing of the dolphinarium caused problems for the owner. He already had enough problems; he would have to increase the size and depth of his pool by 1993 in order to comply with new 'standards' laid down for dolphinaria.

The campaign was handled well. A petition signed by 4,000 people was handed to the council. As spokesperson for the campaign, Bev Cowley spoke with conviction at the meeting. Describing the life of a wild dolphin and comparing it to Rocky's purposeless existence in the crumbling pool, she concluded that 'We firmly believe that if Rocky isn't taken from his existing surroundings and placed in a more humane and natural environment as soon as possible, this concrete box which has been his "home" will become his grave.' It was a victory; 47 out of 50 members voted in favour of withdrawing all publicity for the dolphinarium. The final blow to Morecambe Marineland had been dealt.

Plans for Rocky's release progressed further at the 1990 'Bellerive Symposium on Whales & Dolphins in Captivity' in Geneva, chaired by Prince Sadruddin Aga Khan. A proposal put forward by Ric O'Barry outlined a plan for dolphin rehabilitation. An available site for dolphin release had been found and Rocky could be the first candidate. A major British Sunday newspaper, *The Mail on Sunday* agreed to mount a high-profile appeal for the project with Zoo Check, to be known as 'Into the Blue'.

With the support of several other animal charities, and dozens of celebrities from the worlds of sport, fashion, entertainment and art, the appeal was launched officially on 4 November 1990.

The appeal was an unbelievable success. The British public – always ready to respond to stories of animals and people in trouble – gave generously in order that Rocky could have the chance of a new life. Perhaps they realized that, if successful, Rocky's release would be a symbol of hope for other dolphins – a flagship for the future.

Looking back on the months of work leading up to Rocky's departure from Britain following the appeal, I remember feeling quite daunted by the scale and ambition of the project. Without our team of dedicated staff and volunteers, and their conviction that what we were doing was right, I doubt if we could have coped with the problems and intricacies of the rescue plan. Fourteen-hour days were a regular part of our schedule!

Rocky's owner had generously agreed to give Rocky to the project rather than sell him to another dolphinarium. 'I care more for Rocky than for the money. It's only right he should retire after so long.' British Airways Cargo offered free space in a *747* jumbo jet for Rocky and his veterinary team and handlers. Trade Wind Industries and their conservation branch PRIDE had

RIGHT Rocky and his trainer

> _Betwixt the quarters flows a golden sea;_
> _But foaming surges there in silver play;_
> _The dancing dolphins with their tails divide_
> _The glittering waves, and cut the precious tide;_

VIRGIL
The Aenid. Book VIII

ABOVE Providenciales, an unspoilt, unexploited island of brilliant white beaches fringed by aquamarine waters

provided the 80-acre sea lagoon on Providenciales, an unspoilt, unexploited island of brilliant white beaches fringed by aquamarine waters in the Turks and Caicos islands. Many groups of wild dolphins swim in the seas around these islands – one of the safest places in the world for a retirement and possible release programme.

A leading American veterinary surgeon, Dr Deke Beusse – an expert in the field of cetacean welfare and transportation – was brought over to supervise Rocky's health and well-being, and a team from British Divers Marine Life Rescue gave their invalu-able time and expertise. So far, things were going well.

There was one element, however, that we had overlooked. We had failed to appreciate the extent of the animosity felt by members of the dolphin industry against the release project. This animosity now rose to confront us.

A few days before Rocky was due to fly out,

LEFT The route to a new life

the heating at Morecambe Marineland broke down. The Zoo Check office was alerted and Will Travers instantly arranged for an immediate emergency gas connection. Before this could take place, Rocky's trainer spirited him away to Flamingoland! The problems were just beginning.

A sign that a dolphin is stressed is revealed by an increase in white blood cells. Following the move to Flamingoland, Rocky was found to have a high white blood cell count – probably as a direct result of the transportation from Morecambe – and was considered unfit to travel to Providenciales. It was also implied that he had 'fallen in love' with one of the females in the Flamingoland pool. A more accurate description might have been that Rocky was pleased to have a little company for once, and that the dolphinarium owner was desperate to have a male which might mate with the females.

What had been planned as a straightforward rescue operation was transformed into a metaphorical battleground. However, following this series of delaying tactics, a High Court injunction was served on Flamingoland's owner (he was not the owner of Rocky in any case) to stop him from blocking Rocky's departure any further.

After seven stressful weeks for everybody concerned, Rocky was finally on his way to freedom.

Into the plane, with smiles from vet Richard Kock and Doug Cartlidge

Tender loving care from
warden Lee Chanona
and the team

Rocky in the lagoon

Resting in his sheepskin-lined sling, and covered with a protective coating of lanolin, Rocky seemed calm as his travelling crate was hoisted into the plane, watched every minute of the way by vet Dr Richard Kock and the team. A long 26-hour journey lay ahead of them. The weeks of uncertainty and trauma had been a strain. But, at last, everyone was smiling.

I wonder if Rocky had any sense of *déjà-vu* as he was slipped off his stretcher into the sea after nineteen years in artificial sea-water in a concrete pool? He showed no sign of stiffness or disorientation as he first swam in the medical pen and then in the lagoon sanctuary. Eighty acres must have felt like the world itself after a 38-foot swimming pool, and the tastes and sounds of a natural environment must have stimulated many responses that had lain dormant for so long.

Having rarely vocalized in the dolphin-arium, Rocky let off a whole series of clicks and whistles as he was released into the pen – in between mouthfuls of fish! Watching him streak through the water in a long, straight line, and sensing his stimulation and excitement was a deeply emotional experience for the team. Perhaps especially for the ex-trainers who had also been part of the industry and who were now 'released'.

*The cetaceans ... certainly do not breed well in
dolphinaria; and any reserve that was earmarked for
them would have to be so extensive that they would
hardly be captive at all.*

COLIN TUDGE
Last Animals at the Zoo

The proponents of breeding in concrete pools, who extol them for being 'safe' and far-removed from the 'dangers of the wild', appear to have little understanding of what immense problems are faced by the animals. Breeding is all that seems to matter.

Brighton Dolphinarium had carried out an intensive breeding programme over the years. It is difficult to be precise about numbers, as records were so poorly kept, but between 1968 and 1990, at least six calves were born at Brighton. None have survived. In addition, since 1968, up to 29 adults have either died or 'disappeared'.

Public opinion against the sunless, shoddy establishment, 'home' to Missie and Silver, grew by leaps and bounds in the late 1980s. Following a visit to the dolphinarium, Lucy Maiden began what was at first a one-woman vigil outside the building – a vigil that was to gather momentum. It lead to peaceful but continuous protests and marches – one of which I joined after the death of Missie and Silver's five-month-old calf, Minnie.

A ship's badge modelled on the Arms of
Brighton town

Some members of Brighton Council were deeply unhappy about this situation, which was attracting considerable condemnation and controversial press coverage. But because of loopholes in the Secretary of State's *Standards of Modern Zoo Practice*, the Council was unable to revoke the dolphinarium's licence.

What saved the day for the dolphins was the prospect of having to upgrade the pool to new government standards in 1993, and, more significantly, the pressure of a highly critical public.

The owners of the dolphinarium sold out to Sea Life Centres – whose owners decided not to keep sea mammals at Brighton any longer. The new management felt that Missie and Silver had 'certainly earned their freedom after 36 years between them performing in a concrete box'. They magnanimously gave the dolphins to Into the Blue. Lucy's vigil had not been in vain.

The team accompanying Missie and Silver on their long journey to Providenciales

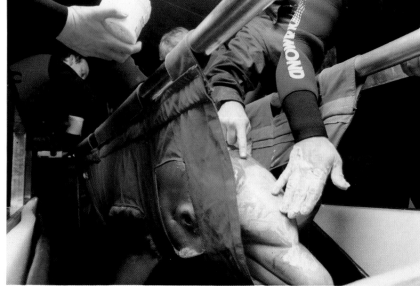

ABOVE Missie's last
moments in the sunless
pool at Brighton
Dolphinarium

ABOVE Silver is
prepared for the long
journey

LEFT At that moment,
nobody was happier
than Gordon

included Gordon Panitzke. Gordon had been part of the team that had captured Missie (then called Baby) in 1969, and that had taken her to Brighton. Now he was watching Missie and Silver (a male captured off Taiwan in 1978) swimming in the medical pen within the lagoon sanctuary. No more artificial behaviour, artificial water, artificial life. At that moment nobody was happier than Gordon.

As he watched, a shape sped through the water and came alongside the pen. Rocky had come to meet his new companions. At this time, nobody knew if a release into the ocean would ever be possible. The present was what mattered. This was the time for healing of dolphin mind and body, for chasing live fish, for racing at speed through the water, for leaping at will, for play. The time for real life to begin again.

Rocky, Missie and Silver in the medical pen. This was the time for healing of dolphin mind and body

Missie and Silver in the lagoon

Several months were to pass before any decision could be made about the dolphins' future. Above all, their health had to be assessed, as had their prowess at catching live fish – integral to their survival in the wild. The dolphins grew in strength and well-being. After only two days, Missie and Silver were bow-riding! After a few weeks, eyes became open and bright, skin problems healed and their limp dorsal fins (a characteristic of most captive dolphins) became erect and firm. No traces of their captive years were visible as they cavorted and dived in their ocean refuge. Everybody was delighted with their progress and began thinking seriously about returning them to the open sea. It was a big step, a big responsibility.

Missie bow-riding

A colleague of Richard Kock's, Dr Barkley Hastings, flew to Providenciales to examine the dolphins. He found them in good health, freeze-branded them on their dorsal fins and increased their food intake in preparation for release. A few weeks later, Rocky, Missie and Silver were transported from the medical pen to an ocean holding pen, 12 miles out to sea. And that is where my son Will and I saw them a few days later.

There was quite a crowd of friends and colleagues with us on the boat – including Angus MacPherson, the feature writer from *The Mail on Sunday*. It had become more than just a 'story' to Angus, and he was as concerned as we all were that everything should go smoothly. As we drew near the release site, I could see the square frame of the pen in the huge expanse of water and, inside it, three curved and shining bodies that intermittently broke the surface of

The dolphin's erect fin, 'shaped like a thorn on a rose'

their little patch of blue. The island nearby was deserted – just sand, grass and windswept shrubs. Around the pen were other boats – the group from the management of the lagoon sanctuary, their film crew and friends. It will be perfect, I thought, when we have all gone and the dolphins can be left in peace!

The morning of the release day was stormy. Thunder rattled and rain pelted down. The release had to be delayed and it was not until 12.35pm that – everyone in position with cameras above and below the water – the gate of the pen was opened.

We had been told it was unlikely that the dolphins would dash out from the pen the moment they saw the barrier was down, and it was not until 1.03pm that Rocky – big, strong Rocky – went through the opening. He went in and out four or five times, as if to encourage the others, but they did not follow his lead straight away. Gaining in confidence, they finally left the pen at 1.45pm. They were all free.

They swam and played around the boats for about two hours, seemingly unstressed and relaxed. It was a totally joyful time. The dolphins stayed around the boats that night, but then quite suddenly disappeared. For six hours. When they returned they were offered fish but seemed totally uninterested, which was most encouraging. It was as if they had just come back to reassure us.

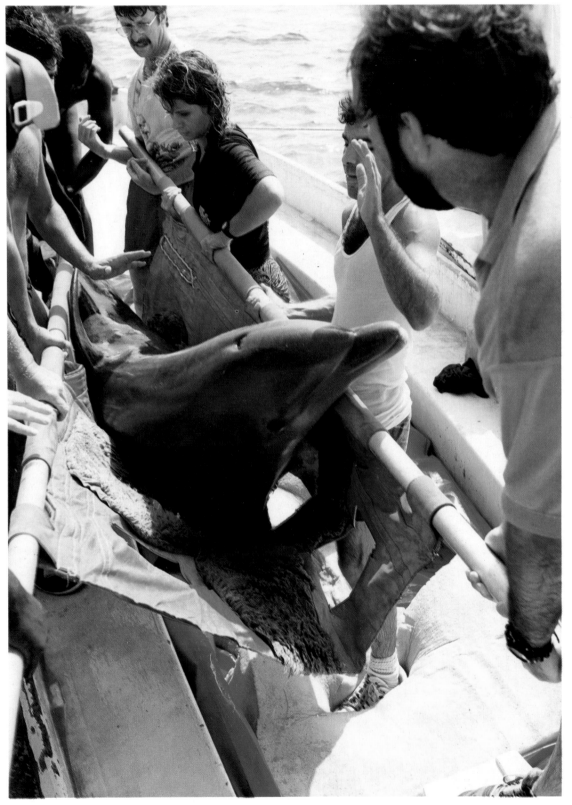

Before Will and I left three days later, Rocky, Missie and Silver had returned twice more. It had been decided that a post-release monitoring period would be maintained for several months. Over a four-month period, there were 25 sightings by the wardens and fishermen. Sometimes the dolphins were together, sometimes they were separate.

For a few days, Silver appeared in the sea near Jojo's territory. He had a few lesions and scars, but these gradually healed. Later that month, when Horace Dobbs was in the Turks and Caicos islands, he was astonished to see a dolphin with an arrow on his dorsal fin pop up near the boat. Silver! According to Horace he was looking fine and, although he stayed around for a while, he was soon off again. The next day he was seen 10 miles away.

Into the Blue is the world's first long-term rehabilitation scheme for dolphins. The second programme is underway – again in the Turks and Caicos islands, but at a different location that will provide facilities for retirement as well as for release.

Rocky, Missie and Silver are taking their chances in the wild. Whatever their fate, they will have had a taste of what it is like to be free and independent. They have proved that rehabilitation and release for long-term captives is not a fanciful dream. As Angus MacPherson put it so well; 'For my part, it may be corny, but I'll always see Rocky as the Neil Armstrong of dolphins. Through the gate to freedom was one small swim for a dolphin. But a giant leap for his kind.'

LEFT Missie leaves
the lagoon for the
ocean pen

LEFT The ocean pen –
the last stop before
freedom

BELOW They were
all free

RIGHT Silver looked fine

For the animal shall not be measured by man. In a world older and more complete than ours, they move finished and complete, gifted with extensions of the senses we have lost or never attained, living by voices we shall never hear.

HENRY BESTON (1888–1968)
The Outermost House

BELOW *Dolphins*
Gary Hodges

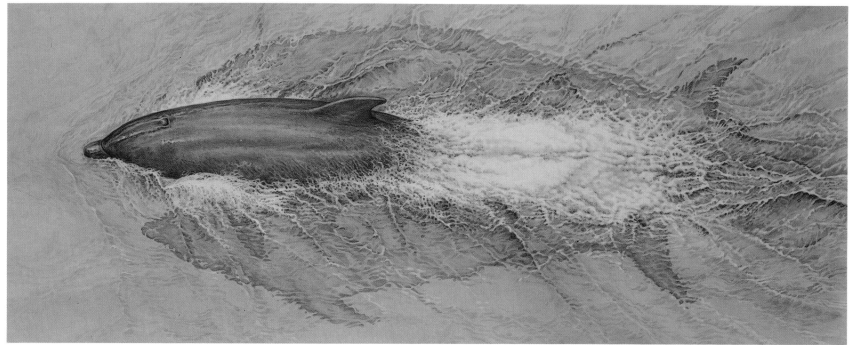

The word 'release' is reverberating around the world. In 1990, Atlantis Marine Park in Western Australia held its last performance. The Japanese-owned dolphinarium, with eight resident dolphins (four of which were born in captivity), reacted to rapidly diminishing public attendances and closed its gates.

Taking a remarkable and unusual decision, the Japanese company decided to fund a rehabilitation project for the dolphins, to be master-minded by marine mammal expert Dr Nick Gales. The project was to run for three years, and the animals were to be returned to the same area from which they had been captured.

The dolphins were moved to a specially constructed pen near to the release area. Seawater was piped into the pen and a gate allowed access from it into a nearby marina, and then into the sea. The usual un-training procedures had been carried out after the closure of the dolphinarium. Nick Gales' account of the release is fascinating:

'For that first day the dolphins were encouraged to swim in and out of the gate following our small boats and to build up confidence with the outside area. This only took 24 hours and, to our surprise, one dolphin, Rajah (the least dominant of our mature males), boldly followed our boat out to sea the very next day. We have all adult dolphins radio tagged so that we can find and follow them in the open ocean. I am now so pleased we used these tags as the dolphins have spread out over 120 nautical miles of coast, and we would have had little chance of finding them without the tags.

'We thought Rajah would follow us back into the pen after his first trip out, but instead he moved off and swam south from the marina. We were able to follow him for several hours and witnessed

Victor Ambrus

several very encouraging interactions with wild dolphins during that period. Sea conditions and lack of daylight prevented us from following him further. The next day we finally heard his radio transmitter some 50 miles south of the marina, but were unable to get a visual sighting.

'A few days later, all but one of our dolphins moved out to sea overnight. We found them just north of the marina and I made the decision to capture the one juvenile female who had remained behind and to take her out to the female group. This female group had her mum in it and I considered that her only real chance of making it in the wild was with her mum.

'That went well and we tracked the whole group (which also included the two dominant males) for some nine hours before nightfall. None of them was interested in our boat, nor were they interested in responding to a special recall we had made that they all responded well to in the pen.'

During the following week, the animals divided up into groups. Two dominant males had moved south and were flourishing, and a mother and her new born calf were also foraging and doing well.

However, Nick was very concerned about some of the others. The three juvenile females had separated from the adults. Two of them had not been seen but one, Echo, was known to have been soliciting food from fishermen. She had lost a little weight and so was eventually caught and returned to the ocean pen.

Rajah had also been brought back as he, too, had lost weight. Rani, a pregnant female, had not been seen, and both she and the two younger females were being searched for. Nick hopes that these dolphins will continue to be monitored until mid-1993.

Nothing living should ever be treated with contempt. Whatever it is that lives, a man, a tree, or a bird, should be touched gently, because the time is short.

ELIZABETH GOUDGE
At the Sign of the Dolphin

Into The Blue Michael Foreman

What of the future? I am often asked about that. 'Where will you find other dolphins?' 'Everywhere' is the answer. All over the world there are dolphins languishing in captivity – in hotels, dolphinaria, circuses, petting pools, research facilities and military establishments. There is already a considerable waiting list of dolphins for the *Into the Blue* rehabilitation centre.

Of course, it would be foolish to pretend that returning any animal to the wild is without problems. Whether it is an oryx, lion, monkey, deer, dove or dolphin, there is always the threat of disease, starvation or attack.

They remind me of children
With a faith so simple,
With a faith so gigantic.

As a delighted child leaps
Into its parent's arms
Trusting it will be caught

So the dolphin leaps
Into the blue arms of the sky.

BRIAN PATTEN
Into the Blue

But wild animals have evolved over millions of years to be – wild. Not to be managed by human beings. Once we were thought to have lived in harmony, at one with nature and its creatures. But now we seem to be caught up in an inexorable momentum to destroy them – and ourselves.

We can no longer 'pass through Paradise in a dream'. It is vanishing before our eyes and at our hands. Before it is gone forever, we must try to rekindle a spiritual awareness, try to recapture a forgotten innocence and to put ourselves in our true perspective. As sharers of the earth, as compassionate protectors – not as masters.

Bibliography

Dolphins, Jacques-Yves Cousteau, trans. Jack F. Bernard (Cassell & Co Ltd, London, 1975)

Behind the Dolphin Smile, Richard O'Barry (Algonquin Books, Chapel Hill, USA, 1989)

Whale Nation, Heathcote Williams (Jonathan Cape, 1988)

Falling for a Dolphin, Heathcote Williams (Jonathan Cape, 1990)

Whales, Dolphins, and Porpoises, ed. Sir Richard Harrison & Dr M. M. Bryden (Weldon Owen (Sydney) Merehurst Ltd, London, 1989)

Dolphins, Their Life and Survival, Michael Donoghue & Annie Wheeler (Blandford, 1990)

Dolphins & Porpoises, Louise Quayle (Headline Book Publishing plc, 1989)

The Remarkable Dolphins of Monkey Mia, Hugh Edwards (Hugh Edwards, W. Australia, 1989)

Star Tales, Ian Ridpath (Lutterworth Press, Cambridge, 1988)

Greenpeace Book of Dolphins, ed. John May (Century Editions, The Random Group, 1990)

Deities and Dolphins, Nelson Glueck (Cassell, 1965)

Encounters with Whales and Dolphins, Wade Doak (Hodder & Stoughton, 1988)

The Dolittle Obsession, Michael Bright (Robson Books Ltd, 1990)

The Rose-Tinted Menagerie, William Johnson (Heretic Books Ltd, 1990)

The Extended Circle, com. Jon Wynne-Tyson (Cardinal, Sphere Books, 1990)

Secrets of the Sea, Carl Proujan (Reader's Digest Assoc. London, 1971)

The Natural History of Whales & Dolphins, Peter G. H. Evans (Christopher Helm, London, 1987)

Historia Animalum, Aristotle; trans. Richard Cresswell (H. G. Bohn, 1862)

The Natural History of Pliny, Plinius Secundus; trans. Bostock & Riley, 1848.

On the Character of Animals, Aelinus; trans. A. F. Schofield (Heinemann, 1958).

The Gaia Atlas of Planet Management, ed. by Norman Myers (Pan Books Ltd, 1985)

Herodotus, Herodotus; trans. A. D. Godley (Heineman, 1920)

The Fables of La Fontaine (Reprinted by Bibliophile Books, 1988)

The Faerie Queene Book II, Spenser (Oxford University Press, 1912)

IUCN Red Data Book (IUCN, Gland, Switzerland & Cambridge, 1991)

Cetaceans in Captivity, Professor George Pilleri (Brain Anatomy Institute, Berne, Switzerland, 1983)

Dolphins in Peril (Midwest Whale Protection publication, USA, Summer 1990)

Bellerive Symposium Report on Whales & Dolphins in Captivity (Geneva, Switzerland, 9-10 July, 1990)

Sonar (magazine of The Whale & Dolphin Conservation Society)

Dolphin (magazine of International Dolphin Watch)

Dolphin Circle (magazine of Dolphin Circle)

Dolphins, Porpoises and Whales – An action plan for the conservation of Biological Diversity 1988-1992, comp. W. F. Perrin, Chairman IUCN/SSC, Cetacean Specialist Group & US Marine Fisheries Service NOAA

Hitchhiker's Guide to the Galaxy, Douglas Adams (Pan Books Ltd, 1979)

Photo Credits

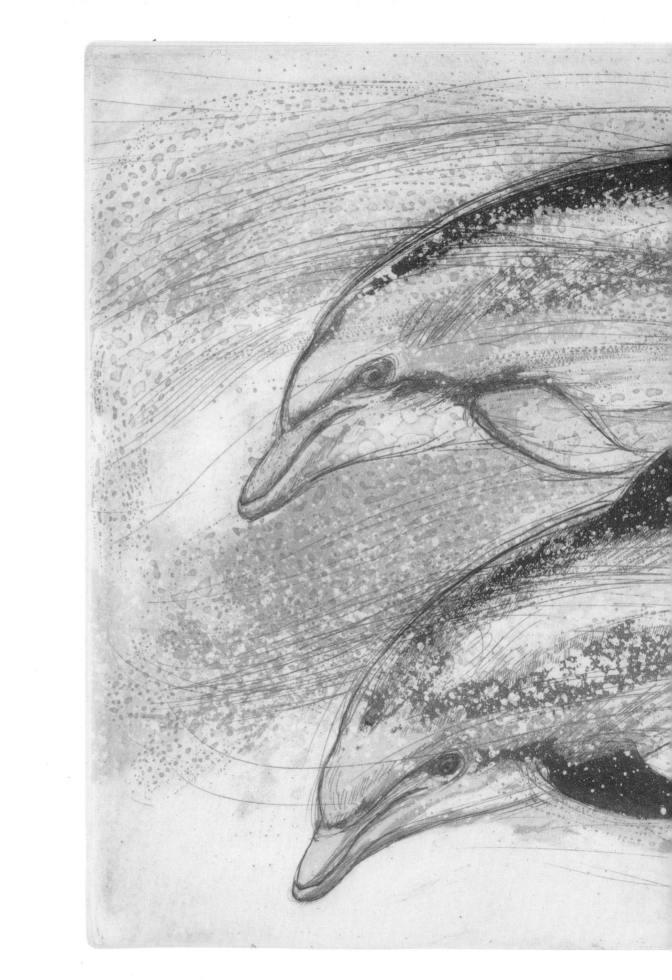